Georgia Odyssey

Georgia Odyssey

SECOND EDITION

James C. Cobb

The University of Georgia Press *Athens & London*
Published in association with the Georgia Humanities Council

© 1997, 2008 by The University of Georgia Press
Athens, Georgia 30602
www.ugapress.org
Published in association with
The Georgia Humanities Council
Atlanta, Georgia 30303
www.georgiahumanities.org
Designed by Walton Harris
Set in 10.5 / 14 Garamond Premier Pro
Printed and bound by Thomson-Shore

The paper in this book meets the guidelines for permanence
and durability of the Committee on Production Guidelines
for Book Longevity of the Council on Library Resources.
Printed in the United States of America
15   14   13   12   11   P   7   6   5   4   3
Library of Congress Cataloging-in-Publication Data

Cobb, James C. (James Charles), 1947–
Georgia odyssey / James C. Cobb. — 2nd ed.
ix, 188 p. ; 21 cm.
"Published in association with the Georgia Humanities Council."
Includes bibliographical references (p. [165]–176) and index.
ISBN-13: 978-0-8203-3050-1 (pbk. : alk. paper)
ISBN-10: 0-8203-3050-7 (pbk. : alk. paper)
1. Georgia—History. I. Title.
F286.C7 2008
975.8—dc22   2008014527

British Library Cataloging-in-Publication Data available

For Thomas G. Dyer

Preface

COUSIN LUTHER COBB was, by all accounts, a perpetually irascible and disgruntled sort, known to complain in wet weather that the rabbits were "miring up in the woods" and in dry weather that his children would "never see rain again." As family legend has it, one day during an especially long dry spell, Cousin Luther was bemoaning the sad state of his cotton crop to his brother James. Taking his brother into the field, Luther declared, "Jimmy, I believe I've got the sorriest cotton in Hart County!" Wary of his brother's mercurial temperament, James made no comment. Luther persisted, however, demanding that James admit that his cotton was the worst he'd ever seen.

Seeing that Luther would not relent, James finally responded, "Well, Luther, I'll have to agree with you. It's pretty sorry alright."

"By God," Luther spat back, "It's better than any you got!"

I love this story not only because it reminds me of the kind of people I come from but also because it illustrates the way a lot of Georgians, including me, have felt about our state over the years. We may voice any number of complaints about it, but others who do the same had best tread lightly in our presence, especially if their criticisms are based on fleeting, impressionistic glimpses from afar rather than up-close and personal experience.

My attitude toward Georgia does not amount to the love-hate relationship traditionally associated with the great southern writers upon whose company I can surely make no claim. It does, however, approximate the feelings expressed by perhaps the greatest of those writers, William Faulkner, who was able to love his backward and beleaguered state of Mississippi because he had come to understand that, in the case of one's homeland, "you don't love because: you love despite; not for the virtues but despite the faults." Such love is unequivocal, but it is not uncritical; it manifests itself just as authentically in addressing the faults as in celebrating the virtues.

A dozen years ago, I was given a chance to sort out my feelings for Georgia in the opening essay of the 1996 *New Georgia Guide*, an ambitious, comprehensive attempt to broaden, deepen, and most of all freshen the perception of Georgia offered in the old 1940 WPA (Works Progress Administration) guide to the state. The response to the essay was quite positive, leading Karen Orchard and the late Malcolm Call to propose that the University of Georgia Press publish the piece, expanded to cover the Olympic experience, as a book. The result was the first edition of *Georgia Odyssey*, which appeared in 1997.

Ten years later, with the first edition in dwindling supply, Nicole Mitchell, Nancy Grayson, and Derek Krissoff of the University of Georgia Press asked me to present an updated version of my brief take on Georgia's history and culture. What follows is my effort to do that in a way that I hope does justice to the facts without totally concealing my sometimes frustrated and disapproving but always deep and genuine affection for my home state.

I am indebted to all the aforementioned persons for affording me this opportunity. I also want to express my thanks to John Inscoe for sharing his vast bibliographic knowledge, to Jason Manthorne for his swift and reliable research assistance, and to my wonderful wife, Lyra Cobb, for her clear and critical editorial eye. The prime mover behind the *New Georgia Guide* project that begat *Georgia Odyssey* was Dr. Thomas G. Dyer, now University Professor Emeritus and Vice

President for Instruction Emeritus at the University of Georgia. In the course of a truly distinguished career, Tom has led, supported, sustained, and otherwise made possible more good things for the University of Georgia and the people of the state in general than anybody I know. In addition to his innumerable administrative contributions, he is also a scholar of great renown, whose writings include an acclaimed history of the University of Georgia and *Secret Yankees: The Union Circle in Confederate Atlanta*, a pathbreaking study of a little-known or acknowledged Unionist community in Civil War Atlanta.

On a personal note, I don't know if there are truly *no* friends like old friends, but I do know that there are *few* friends of any vintage like Tom Dyer. We met as graduate students at the University of Georgia in 1972, and over the intervening years he has offered unfailingly wise counsel and has done more thoughtful, helpful, and courageous things on my behalf than I could ever recount, and, in fact, has probably done even more of these than I know. His intelligence, integrity, and rich sense of humor are legendary not only around Athens but across the state. Although he was born in Missouri (and therefore persists in thinking he knows more about farming than I do), Tom Dyer is, in the best sense of the term, one of the finest Georgians I have been blessed to know. It seems more than fitting, therefore, that this book be dedicated to him.

Georgia Odyssey

INTRODUCTION

On his frequent visits to his Little White House at Warm Springs, President Franklin D. Roosevelt repeatedly expressed his deep affection for Georgia and its people, a sentiment that the overwhelming majority of the citizens of his "adopted" state seemed to reciprocate. Yet when Roosevelt attacked incumbent U.S. senator Walter F. George as an opponent of the New Deal and called on Georgia voters to oust George in 1938, he was soundly rebuffed. Aware of FDR's personal popularity within the state, a visiting journalist asked a grizzled old South Georgia tobacco farmer to explain this outcome. Without hesitation, the old man replied defiantly, "We Georgians are Georgian as hell!" Whatever else it encompassed, his sense of what it meant to be Georgian suggested an innate distrust of all outsiders and a near-visceral hostility to any changes they might propose, feelings that remained very much alive (and inclined to kicking) some three generations after the end of Reconstruction.

Seventy years after the old fellow's pronouncement, it would be foolhardy indeed for a person to suggest that he or she knows what it means to be Georgian, much less "Georgian as hell!" Likewise, not many of today's Georgians are likely to recognize themselves in the first few pages of the 1940 Works Progress Administration's *Georgia: A Guide to Its Towns and Countryside*: "The average Georgian votes the Democratic ticket, attends the Baptist or Methodist church, goes home to midday dinner, relies greatly on high cotton prices and is so good a family *man* that *he* flings wide *his* doors to even the most distant of *his* wife's cousins' cousins. . . . However cool *he* may be toward the cause of Negro education, the Georgian is usually kind to *his* own servants and not a little apprehensive of hurting their feelings" (italics mine).

Save perhaps for their religious preferences, Georgians have changed a great deal. Typically, a lot more of them than not now vote Republican about as faithfully as they attend church. Not many of them go home to a midday meal, but if they do, they are likely to call it lunch rather than dinner. Likewise, relatively few Georgians exhibit much curiosity at all about cotton prices anymore. Finally, and most important, we now recognize not only that there are both male and female Georgians but that Georgians come in more than one color as well.

In the wake of more than half a century of dramatic changes, even the most reckless essayist would know better than to refer to the "average" Georgian, let alone discuss his or her lifestyle or values. Yet whether we are lifelong residents, homesick expatriates, or fast-assimilating newcomers, a great many of us persist in identifying ourselves as Georgians, believing that we know what this means to us even if that meaning may not be the same for everybody else. Our differences notwithstanding, however, what all self-designated Georgians share either by birthright or by adoption is a common past. Not all of that past is pretty or pleasant to recall (whose is?), but any attempt to understand the character and personality of contemporary Georgia must take into account its sometimes disturbing, sometimes appealing, but always rich and eventful historical odyssey.

GEORGIA AS A COLONY

As we shall soon see, having absorbed their fair share of critical scrutiny, plus a good bit of plain old abuse over the years, Georgians are a mite sensitive about the way they and their state are perceived. As a result, we may as well deal with it right now, at the beginning. Contrary to what you may have heard, read, or been taught, Georgia was not settled by convicts of any sort. Even otherwise amiable Georgians are downright touchy on this point. (As a native Georgian teaching U.S. history to northern college freshmen, I used to inform my students that when I heard anyone repeat the outrageous falsehood that Georgians are descended from thieves and murderers, it made me so mad that I wanted to shoot him or at least take his wallet.)

Those familiar with Georgia's history as a European outpost know that it actually began not with English convicts but with Spanish explorers and missionaries whose first contact with the area came nearly two centuries before Georgia was chartered as a British colony. Hernando de Soto led the first European expedition into the state's interior in 1540, but despite Spain's subsequent efforts to establish a foothold in what would later be coastal and southeastern Georgia, English incursions began shortly after the founding of Jamestown in 1607 and became more frequent and intense after the nearby Carolina colony was established in 1670. Still, although Georgia received its charter in 1732, it was not until a decade later that forces under Georgia's founder, James Edward Oglethorpe, sealed Georgia's future as part of the British Empire by repulsing the Spanish at the Battle of Bloody Marsh on St. Simons Island.

Along with the twenty other trustees to whom Georgia's royal charter was granted, Oglethorpe had hoped, initially at least, to promote penal reform and the relocation of the homeless and downtrodden to an idyllic New World wilderness offering "fertile lands sufficient to subsist all the useless poor in England." Like most proponents of noble experiments, Oglethorpe was given to exaggeration. He described Georgia as "always serene, pleasant, and temperate, never subject to excessive heat or cold, nor to sudden changes; the winter is regular and short, and the summer cool'd with refreshing breezes." Georgia was, in short, "a lush, Edenic paradise, capable of producing almost every thing in wonderful quantities."

Charged with overseeing the settlement of Georgia and ensuring its growth, the trustees reasoned that because it occupied roughly the same latitude as China, Persia, and the Madeira Islands, the new colony could supply the silks and wines that England was currently forced to purchase from producers outside the British Empire. Georgia, then, seemed to offer that most rare and wonderful of coincidences, an opportunity to do what was morally good, serve the national interest, and make a buck in the bargain. Moreover, populated by sturdy and sober yeomen and tradesmen — lawyers were banned as were slavery, Catholicism, and hard liquor — Georgia would provide an excellent defensive perimeter for the prosperous colony of South Carolina, which was attracting altogether too much attention from the Spanish in Florida.

It was small wonder that many investors and proponents found the Georgia experiment irresistible; nor was it surprising that this seemingly ideal combination of philanthropy, capitalism, and national interest went awry. There was no shortage of people wanting to go to Georgia, and because those chosen as the colony's initial settlers would receive a host of benefits, including free passage, fifty acres of land, and supplies and foodstuffs for a year, they were screened carefully — so carefully, in fact, that the first Georgians were perhaps the most selectively chosen group of colonists to come to British North America. They came from the ranks of small businessmen, tradesmen, and unemployed laborers, representing what historian Phinizy Spalding described as a "London in microcosm" with the "large debtor element" notably underrepresented and nearly absent altogether. Oglethorpe and the trustees did bend colonial policy a bit by welcoming Jews and other persecuted religious minorities like the Lutheran Salzburgers, who established a settlement at Ebenezer in what later became Effingham County.

The colony's economic future hardly went as planned either. The mulberry trees that grew wild throughout Georgia proved unsuitable for silk production, but even when colonists secured the proper variety of trees, silkworms found the colony's cold snaps a bit too nippy for their tastes. Meanwhile, those who have sampled the fruits of such modern vineyards as are compatible with the local climate and soils will have little difficulty understanding why Georgia never became the colonial equivalent of the Napa Valley.

Colonial Georgia suffered an unfavorable balance of trade because its production of goods for export (hampered to some extent by the trustees' regulations) was too feeble to finance the importation of goods from abroad. Restrictions on rum and landholding were eventually relaxed, but the young colony languished, remaining the smallest and poorest British royal possession in North America. In later generations, Georgians would balk at admitting that their state had begun as a buffer for South Carolina. Likewise, they would not rush to concede that Georgia ultimately survived by becoming more like South Carolina. Yet early on, discontented Georgians began to cast envious eyes on the wealth and lifestyles of the Carolina rice planters whose crops provided a major export commodity that supported a much livelier commerce than Georgia enjoyed.

Georgia's trustees had warned steadfastly against slavery and single-crop plantation farming, but their moralistic arguments were no match for the avarice and ambition of their critics — especially the prominent members of Savannah's business community, not to speak of George Whitefield, the colony's leading minister of the gospel. The arguments of the proslavery faction were ably summarized by Thomas Stephens, whose father was actually secretary to the trustees and their chief agent in Georgia:

And indeed the extraordinary Heats here, the extraordinary Expences in maintaining, hiring and procuring White Servants, the extraordinary Difficulty and Danger there is in clearing the Lands, attending and Manufacturing the Crops, working in the Fields in Summer, and the poor Returns of Indian Corn, Pease and Potatoes, which are as yet the only chief Produces of the Land there, make it indisputably impossible for White Men alone to carry on Planting to any good Purpose.... The poor People of Georgia, may as well think of becoming Negroes themselves (from whose Condition at present they seem not to be far removed) as of hoping to be ever able to live without them; and they ought best to know, and most to be believed, who have made the Experiment.

Ignoring protests that "those folk who wanted to bring in Negroes . . . would put an end to Men's Work," the proslavery advocates pushed their case until they got their way in 1750. Two years later, when Georgia became a royal colony after the trustees returned their charter to the Crown, the ill-fated efforts to maintain it as a morally pristine backwoods utopia came to an end.

By 1760 more than one-third of Georgia's population were slaves, and by the eve of the American Revolution, the figure was nearly one-half. James Wright, who became the royal governor in 1760, had held a variety of positions in the South Carolina bureaucracy, and hence he led the way in the Carolina-ization of Georgia. Governor Wright played a key role in Georgia's physical growth as well, negotiating treaties with nearby Indians that increased the colony's land area approximately fivefold. Meanwhile, Georgia's population increased almost tenfold in the 1750s and 1760s, and expanded production of rice (amounting to some twenty thousand barrels on the eve of the Revolution) and indigo spurred the colony's economic upturn. Though South Carolina had a head start, by 1770 Georgia was beginning to contribute its share to the growing value of American colonial exports and was perhaps on its way to becoming another jewel in the crown of British mercantilism.

Although the trustees had been specifically forbidden to own land, hold office, or profit from the colony in any way, their successors in the royal government chafed under no such restraints. Indeed, Governor Wright and his cohorts were soon among the colony's most affluent landowners and slaveholders. By 1773, sixty people owned at least twenty-five hundred acres each, and together they held more than 50 percent of the colony's slaves. Colonial policies encouraging land speculation facilitated this consolidation of wealth, while ambitious yeomen faced major financial obstacles in becoming rice or indigo planters. As time passed, the small farmers of Georgia saw themselves steadily losing ground relative to the affluent planter minority, and they blamed their difficulties on the royal government that seemed so acutely attuned to planter interests. Colonial officials responded with open contempt; Colonial Council president James Habersham described their critics to Governor Wright as the people who were "really what you and I understand as Crackers."

As this reference suggests, Georgians can assert a long-standing claim on, as one writer described it, "one of the oldest pejoratives in America." In recent years, the term *Cracker* has enjoyed widespread usage as a derogatory reference to whites — usually poor whites — employed primarily by blacks. Historically, however, Crackers suffered the abuse and slights of a number of socially superior whites, both northern and southern in origin. Ethnically, the original, prototypical Crackers were probably of Scotch-Irish descent. Dr. Samuel Johnson had defined a Cracker in 1755 as a "noisy, boasting fellow." Backcountry Crackers enjoyed a reciprocally disdainful relationship with their Anglican, low-country detractors. In 1775 Rev. Charles Woodmason, an English-born Anglican missionary, quickly became disgusted with the uncouth Crackers who disrupted his sermons and seemed inclined to "bluster and make a Noise about a Turd." Crackers, Woodmason believed, behaved so believing "they have a Right because they are Americans — born to do as they please . . . to any Body." As time passed, the stereotype of Cracker as backwoods boaster was augmented by the practice of "cracking" corn to produce the meal for corn bread, which was the staple of the Cracker diet. A somewhat less opprobrious derivation came from "whip-crackers," herdsmen who used long whips tapered to a cracker to drive their cattle in the unfenced forests and free ranges of antebellum Georgia and Florida. Cracker herdsmen were often people of considerably better economic circumstances than appearances might have suggested, but the term remained a derisive one, especially among blacks, who often ridiculed the "white trash" who occupied the scrub lands around the plantations and who, after emancipation, proved to be their major antagonists.

The Cracker/planter schism grew more pronounced as Georgia drifted into the American Revolution. *Drifted* is an appropriate term because Georgia played a relatively minor role in the conflict. Georgia was the only colony to comply with the Stamp Act, and it sent no official delegation to the First Continental Congress. Georgia's emergent political leaders reached no firm consensus on the question of independence, and within the colony, matters of faction and in-group/out-group squabbling remained paramount. Defenders of the Crown faced opposition from a coalition largely drawn from the Savannah area's "Christ Church" faction consisting of socially elite but out-of-power planters and merchants and the "country" faction consisting of non-Anglican upcountry planters and farmers and artisans from the towns. This coalition was loose at best, as exemplified by the fatal shooting in a duel of Button Gwinnett, a volatile leader of the country faction, at the hands of Lachlan McIntosh, a member of the more conservative Christ Church faction. Naturally, when the British showed up and occupied Savannah in 1778, matters became even messier.

War may be a misleading term for the American Revolution as it played out in Georgia, for it implies a degree of organization and structure seldom observed in the thirteenth colony during the conflict. While it may not have been war, it was certainly bloody. With Tories in control of Savannah and the low-country plantation areas, fighting raged in the backwoods, where guerrilla activity amounted less to pitched battles and sieges than to skirmishes, ambushes, lynchings, and cold-blooded murder.

From this context emerged one of Georgia's most heroic and mythologized historical figures, Nancy Morgan Hart, a backcountry patriot of the first order, who at the time of the Revolution lived in the Broad River wilderness of present-day Elbert County with her husband, Benjamin Hart. Legend and lore have it that Nancy was anything but the stereotypical southern belle. In 1825 a Milledgeville newspaper offered this description:

> In altitude, Mrs. Hart was almost Patagonian, remarkably well-limbed and muscular, and marked by nature with prominent features. She possessed none of those graces of motion which a poetical eye might see in the heave of the ocean wave or in the change of the summer cloud; nor did her cheeks — I will not speak of her nose — exhibit the rosy tints which dwell on the brow of the evening or play on the gilded bow. No one claims for her throat that it was lined with fiddle strings. That dreadful scourge of beauty, the small-pox had set its seal upon her face. She was called a hard swearer, was cross-eyed and coarse-grained, but was nevertheless a sharp-shooter.

Legend has it that local Indians stood so in awe of Nancy that they named a stream near her cabin "War Woman Creek." In Nancy's case, the truth may indeed be stranger than fiction and thus all the harder to verify, but her most documentable exploit went something like this:

Disdaining flight in the face of the British advance into the hinterlands from Augusta and Savannah, Nancy had made her cabin a refuge for patriots who sought to harass the local Tory populations. When six Tories descended upon her cabin and accosted her about this, she feigned submission and appeared to comply with their demands to prepare a meal for them. As she did so, she dispatched her daughter Sukey to the spring, ostensibly for water but actually to blow the conch shell kept there to summon help when it was needed.

Meanwhile, as the smell of turkey, venison, and hoecake filled the cabin, the Tories broke out a jug of whiskey and began to pass it around, even asking an all-too-amenable Nancy to enjoy a swig or two. As the mood grew mellower, the men failed to notice that Nancy was pushing their muskets out through cracks in her cabin wall. When they finally realized what she was doing, she immediately shouldered a musket and demanded that they "surrender their damned Tory carcasses to a Whig woman." Nancy's crossed eyes presented her Tory captors-turned-captives with a dilemma. It was difficult to tell where her gaze actually fell, as one of them learned when he sought to make a furtive move for his musket and paid for his mistake with his life. A quick-thinking Sukey promptly passed her mama another musket, and after a second Tory fell, the remainder thought better of such foolhardiness. Eventually Benjamin Hart arrived and quite possibly earned his lasting reputation as a wimp by suggesting that the Tories be shot. The fiery Nancy objected vociferously, insisting on hanging the men on the spot.

Though most of Nancy's exploits are totally unsubstantiated, on December 12, 1912, a gang of workers grading a railroad discovered six skeletons in shallow graves about a half mile from the apparent site of Nancy's cabin. This discovery may or may not have substantiated Nancy Hart's most famous escapade, but in this case, as in not a few others where Georgians are concerned, image and symbolism count far more than reality. Nancy Hart was a fitting symbol of the white population of upcountry Georgia in the Revolutionary era. Crude, illiterate, no strangers to hardship or conflict, they were survivors, and the longer they survived, the more social and political momentum they gained.

OPPORTUNITY AND SLAVERY IN
ANTEBELLUM GEORGIA

Because royal forces remained in control of the more established population centers for much of the Revolutionary conflict, the backcountry naturally gained independence and influence during this period. With political power redistributed, men like Elijah Clark, the hero of many a backcountry skirmish, rose to prominence. Although the impact of the confiscation of Tory property is easily exaggerated, it helped to reshuffle Georgia's economic hierarchy, as did the disruption of agriculture and commerce brought on by nearly seven years of armed conflict. British bounties on the production of indigo were gone forever, and rice production remained below prewar levels for nearly twenty years.

As the once-mighty fell, the once-lowly rose. Public land policy was a boon to the ambitions of an upwardly mobile yeomanry. Fees were minimal, and heads of household could claim as much as two hundred acres of land for themselves with additional allowances for their dependents and for up to ten slaves. A desperate Revolutionary government had offered generous land bounties to any white man who had fought for the patriot cause in Georgia, including not only non-Georgians but even British deserters. As a result, few white males failed to qualify for free land.

So-called treaties with various Indian tribes made more land available and helped to unleash a veritable orgy of speculation and corruption culminating in the 1795 Yazoo Land Fraud, in which four land companies bribed legislators to approve their acquisition of 35 million acres (nearly 60 percent of the land area that now constitutes Alabama and Mississippi) at the cost of only five hundred thousand dollars. In the wake of this scandal, the legislature quickly shifted to a lottery system that made land available at about seven cents per acre. Under this new plan, more than one hundred thousand individuals and families laid claim to approximately three-fourths of Georgia's land.

After the Yazoo fraud, Governor James Jackson opened the negotiations that led in 1802 to the ceding of the western lands beyond the Chattahoochee to the federal government. This action allowed Alabama and Mississippi to escape the fate of being part of Georgia, and in the bargain, Georgia acquired two neighbors for whom its residents would in years to come thank God again and again. As part of the cession agreement, Georgia's leaders secured a promise that all remaining Indian land claims in Georgia would be erased as soon as was feasible. Andrew Jackson's victory over the Creeks in the War of 1812 helped to facilitate this process, and under pressure from land-hungry Georgians, the state's officials mounted and maintained a relentless campaign of harassment and legal and political coercion until 1838 when the last sizable contingent of Cherokees, Georgia's only remaining native people, was marched along the Trail of Tears to Oklahoma.

The removal of the Cherokees was one of the most shameful chapters in the state's history, one that revealed the rapacity and brutality that lay behind the emerging economic and social order in antebellum Georgia. John G. Burnett, a soldier who served as an interpreter, was a sad witness to what he called "the execution of the most brutal order in the History of American Warfare." Burnett remembered seeing helpless Cherokees arrested and dragged from their homes and driven at bayonet point into the stockades. "And in the chill of a drizzling rain on an October morning, I saw them loaded like cattle or sheep into six hundred and forty-five wagons and started toward the West. . . . Many of these helpless people did not have blankets, and many of them had been driven from home barefooted. . . . The sufferings of the Cherokees were awful. The trail of the exiles was a trail of death."

In the half century following the Revolution, Georgia emerged as a social, economic, and political paradox as its leaders gave both rhetorical and legal sanction to the promotion and extension of liberty, democracy, and opportunity, even as they increasingly acknowledged the state's growing dependence on slavery. By 1789 all taxpayers (including women in theory though not in practice) were entitled to vote. The state had a popularly elected two-house legislature, and opinion leaned ever more heavily toward popular election of all public officials. The new constitution of 1798, however, acknowledged federal precedent by calculating a county's representation in the legislature according to a formula whereby five slaves were deemed the equivalent of three white constituents. This move reflected not only the resurgence of the old plantation counties, but the spread of slavery into the upcountry as well.

The pivotal event in this trend was, of course, the appearance of a viable cotton gin, a machine, developed by Yankee tutor Eli Whitney on a plantation near Washington, Georgia, that separated cotton fiber from the seeds and, thereby, made it feasible to grow hardier varieties of the plant in hitherto unsuitable upland areas and in larger quantities than was possible when the fiber and seeds had to be separated by hand. The impact of the cotton gin may be measured by comparing Georgia's cotton production in 1791 (one thousand bales) with its output in 1801 (twenty thousand bales). Georgia was soon leading the world in cotton production, which increased about 10 percent a year from 1825 to 1860, largely in response to the demands of the rapidly expanding English textile industry. As incessant planting led to depleted soils, the center of southern cotton production began to shift toward the newer, more fertile southwestern states. Still, with the insatiable looms of Lancaster to feed, cotton was paying for two-thirds of all American imports, and as the nation's fourth-leading producer of cotton in 1860, Georgia remained a pivotal player in the national and international economy.

The more cotton Georgia planters grew, the more slaves they needed, and a slave population of just under thirty thousand in 1790 had swollen to almost sixty thousand by 1800 and to well over a hundred thousand by 1810. On the eve of the Civil War, nearly a half million slaves, perhaps 75 percent of them concentrated in the fertile Black Belt (a strip of land which ran roughly across the middle third of the state), constituted 44 percent of the state's total population.

The cotton boom not only revitalized slavery, but it also democratized slave ownership, at least for a time, as yeomen farmers managed to acquire both land and slaves. As historian Numan Bartley observed, "After almost a century of frequent strife and social conflict, white Georgians seemed to have arrived at a consensus that rested on the production of the white staple with black labor on land that had been taken from red people." Although Georgia had more slaves and slaveholders than any state save Virginia, in 1860 fewer than a third of Georgia's adult white males actually owned slaves, and almost half of these owned fewer than six. Overall, only 15 percent of the state's slaveholders owned twenty or more slaves. These figures put slaveholders in a decided minority within the white population, but they were an exceedingly powerful minority whose political clout extended well beyond what their numbers on the census pages would suggest. In both 1850 and 1860, more than two-thirds of the seats in the state legislature were held by men who owned slaves, nearly half of them twenty or more.

In the late nineteenth and early twentieth centuries, white Georgians would include in their reminiscences of the slavery era recollections of the happy, contented retainers who seemingly toiled without fatigue, sang rather than sweated, and generally bore their enslavement without frustration or resentment. This imagery was of great psychological value to whites. It assuaged their guilt over slavery and ultimately reaffirmed the wisdom of the Jim Crow system. It even proved valuable to the would-be architects of the New South who, in their search for popular acceptance, seemed at every turn to invoke the glories of the Old South. That this mythology was patently implausible seemed to make little difference. Certainly, ample evidence to the contrary abounds in interviews with former slaves conducted by WPA (Works Progress Administration) workers during the New Deal. Born in Georgia in 1844, William Colbert recalled the story of his brother January, who slipped away to see a woman on another plantation. When he was caught, January's owner tied him to a pine tree and announced:

"Now, nigger, I'm goin' to teach you some sense."

Wid dat he started layin' on de lashes. January was a big fine lookin' nigger, de finest I ever seed. He wuz jus four years older dan me, an' when de massa begin a beatin' him, January never said a word. De massa got madder and madder kaze he couldn't make January holla.

"What's de matter wid you, nigger?" he say. "Don't it hurt?"

January, he never said nothin', and de massa keep a beatin' till little streams of blood started flowin' down January's chest, but he never holler. His lips was a quiverin' and his body wuz a shakin', but his mouff it neber open; and all de while I sat on my mammy's and pappy's steps a cryin'. De niggers wuz all gathered about and some uv 'em couldn't stand it; dey hadda go inside dere cabins. Atter while,

January, he couldn't stand it no longer hisself, and he say in a hoarse, loud whisper: "Massa, Massa, Have Mercy on Dis Poor Nigger!"

Not all masters were as cruel as January's, but the potential for such brutality was always there in the slaveholding society of early nineteenth-century Georgia. Though many of Georgia's slaveholders were quick to take on the airs and trappings of aristocracy, most of them sprang from humble or, at best, modest origins. Margaret Mitchell captured quite well the origins and rapid rise of many a Georgia planter in her *Gone with the Wind* depiction of the short but swaggering, "loud mouthed and bull headed" Gerald O'Hara. "With the deep hunger of an Irishman who has been a tenant on the lands his people once had owned and hunted," Gerald longed with "a ruthless singleness of purpose" to have "his own house, his own plantation, his own horse and his own slaves. And here in this new country . . . he intended to have them."

Chafing in the employ of his brothers in Savannah, Gerald capitalized on two of his prime assets, his facility at poker and his "steady head for whiskey," to become the owner of a gone-to-seed plantation. With what he could borrow from his brothers and secure from mortgaging the land, he bought a few hands and moved into the old overseer's place while he dreamed of a great white house to replace the one that had burned down a few years earlier. Clearing fields and planting cotton and borrowing more money and buying more slaves and land, "little, hardheaded blustering Gerald" soon had his dream house and even won social acceptance when the lordly Mrs. Wilkes conceded that despite his "rough tongue . . . he is a gentleman." And what was the educational and cultural pedigree of this newly anointed gentleman? He could read, write, and cipher, but "there his book knowledge stopped. The only Latin he knew was the responses of the Mass and the only history, the manifold wrongs of Ireland. . . . After all, what need had he of these things in a new country where the most ignorant of bogtrotters had made great fortunes? in this country which asked only that a man be strong and unafraid of work?"

New Hampshire native Emily Pillsbury was one of many critical and condescending northern visitors who seized on the educational deficiencies of the so-called planter aristocracy in antebellum Georgia. "To those educated in New England, the ignorance that is seen in many portions of the northern part of Georgia is truly astonishing; many cannot read a word, or write their own name. I have had merchants say, that in transacting business with many men of great wealth, they have found them obliged to use a mark for their signature."

Like so many northern observers, Pillsbury often confused poor whites with the South's sizable body of independent yeoman farmers. She gave little credit to Georgia's nonslaveholding whites for their independence and self-sufficiency, noting with disapproval that "besides coffee they seldom use any thing that is not the product of their own industry."

In addition to their victimization at the hands of the planters and their inherited inclinations to poverty, Pillsbury traced the plight of Georgia's lower-class whites to the absence of a system of common schools. It was here that she drew the sharpest and perhaps most ironic distinction between Georgia with its "deplorable state of ignorance" and her native New England: "At that age when the youth of the North are confined at hard lessons for six hours a day from one season to another, these [Georgia] children are wasting the spring of their lives, in the fields and woods, climbing trees, robbing birds' nests, or breaking up the haunts of squirrels, and engaged in every such kind of mischief, enough of which is always to be found for idle hands to do."

"Mischief" was hardly confined to children in antebellum Georgia. In 1835, humorist Augustus Baldwin Longstreet described a violent encounter between Billy Stallings and Bob Durham, who were believed by their Georgia peers to be "the very best men in the country," which, as Longstreet explained, "means they could flog any other two men in the county." Each man had his own following, and though there was much agitated speculation as to which of these two "best" men was actually the better, the fisticuffs-loving locals were much frustrated because the two actually got along quite well, despite the best efforts of one Ransy Sniffle, who, in Longstreet's words, "never seemed fairly alive, except when he was witnessing, fomenting, or talking about a fight." Whereas Billy and Bob were physical specimens of the first rank, Ransy's appearance reflected a childhood in which he had "fed copiously upon red clay and blackberries," the result being a "complexion that a corpse would have disdained to own." In height, Ransy stood "just five feet nothing, while his average weight in blackberry season [was] ninety five."

Ransy finally succeeded in bringing Billy and Bob to blows by reporting to Bob on Billy's disrespectful conduct toward Bob's wife. The ensuing combat, "a fair fight," led to incredible carnage. At its end, Billy "presented a hideous spectacle. About a third of his nose at the lower extremity was bitten off, and his face was so swelled and bruised, that it was difficult to discover in it anything of the human visage." Meanwhile, the "victor," Bob, was missing his entire left ear as well as a large chunk of cheek and the middle finger of his left hand, which he had opted to abandon between the clenched teeth of the determined Billy.

Longstreet's account was more caricature than pure fiction. A century later, W. J. Cash neatly summarized the aims and aspirations of many a frontier-bred Georgian when he wrote, "To stand on his head in a bar, to toss down a pint of raw whiskey at a gulp, to fiddle and dance all night, to bite off the nose or gouge out the eye of a favorite enemy, to fight hard and love harder than the next man, to be known eventually far and wide as a hell of a fellow — such would be his focus." Not surprisingly, such behavior made a less-than-favorable impression on visitors to antebellum Georgia. A staid New Englander complained of being "greatly annoyed in the middle of the night by the swearing and vociferation of a number of young men who had been drinking. I do not think I have heard so much swearing, indicating habits of the grossest profaneness at any public house where I have stopped within the last 20 years. There is great reason to fear that Georgia is preeminent in this vice."

Lest such uncouth behavior be attributed solely to the crude country folk, Cash observed that "what is true of the poor white was true in a fashion of the planter and yeoman farmer as well." Anyone who doubts Cash's sweeping generalization need only take note of the rambunctiousness of the sons of Georgia's planters as manifested in the disciplinary records of the University of Georgia. Drunkenness, gambling, and reckless discharging of firearms were constant occurrences, and fighting and armed conflict were alarmingly common. In 1831 an argument reportedly developed between two students, one of whom announced to the other, "If you will go down into the woods, I'll whip you like hell." When the other replied, "This is as good a place as any other," the former accommodated him by stabbing him. (Both students were expelled, then subsequently reinstated.)

Clearly, the propensity for violence had little to do with social standing or intellectual ability. Eventually dismissed from the university, the quick-witted Robert Toombs was a notorious rule breaker and mayhem maker. Pursuing a long-standing feud with two fellow students, Toombs attacked them at various times, wielding a knife, a hatchet, and a pistol. A fiery orator who went on to serve as a U.S. senator and a Confederate general, Toombs became one of Georgia's earliest and most ardent advocates of secession.

Although it pains many Georgians to admit it (and, hence, many still refuse to), the central issue that ultimately drove their deeply divided state from the Union and propelled it into the bloody and economically ruinous conflict, known locally as the War between the States, was the future of slavery. Orators like Toombs may have invoked the principles of states' rights and an overheated sense of individual, state, and regional honor, but Toombs also owned 170 slaves and some two thousand acres of improved land in 1860 and was, in essence, living the white Georgian's version of the American Dream.

For many, this fantasy was well worth fighting for. As early as 1848, for example, a Georgia planter who owned just ten prime field hands was wealthier than all but 1 percent of the citizens of Boston. With an average per capita value of $900 in 1860, slaves represented a source of wealth far more important than the cotton they cultivated or the land on which that cotton grew. The average slaveholder in Georgia was five times wealthier than the average northerner, and a white Georgian who owned but two slaves and nothing else was at least as well off financially as the average northerner. Georgia's largest slaveholders were some of the richest people not only in the nation but in the world. At the time of his death in 1859, Joseph Bond owned eight plantations (six in Dougherty County and two in Lee) and five hundred slaves, and his estimated net worth exceeded a million dollars. In 1858 his plantations had yielded a cotton crop worth $100,000.

Slaveholding meant both wealth and status, and hence, lawyers, doctors, merchants, and anyone else who could do so moved quickly to purchase slaves, acquire land, and thereby assume a primary identity as a "planter." Not surprisingly, the mania for slaveholding resulted in as much as half of Georgia's total wealth being invested in slaves. At approximately $416 million, the estimated aggregate value of slave property in 1860 was nearly forty times that of the state's total investment in manufacturing.

It did not trouble Scarlett O'Hara in the least when she realized that "she'd never seen a factory or known anyone who had seen a factory," but the consequences of Georgians' obsession with slaveowning were serious indeed. In a real sense, slaves were highly mobile capital, and their owners were also highly mobile capitalists. The image of the O'Haras' unshakable ties to Tara may have made for excellent melodrama, but as history, it was generally unrepresentative. By the late antebellum period, continuous cotton cultivation had largely exhausted the soil in many of the old cotton counties to the north and west of Augusta, and many of the area's largest slaveholders had relocated to the still wild and frontierlike counties around Columbus. The profitability of slavery and the mobility of slaveholders combined to stunt the expansion and diversification of urban or small-town economies. Slaveholders had little incentive to transfer lucrative investments in slaves to fledgling businesses and industrial enterprises when they had no tangible stake in the local community per se. As a critical northern visitor, Frederick Law Olmsted observed that when a southern planter was asked about his investments, "he will point in reply, not to dwellings, libraries, churches, school-houses, mills, railroads, or anything of the kind; he will point to his Negroes — to almost nothing else."

We should keep in mind that however shortsighted it may seem in retrospect, the overwhelming concentration of Georgia capital in slaves was not at all irrational, in the purely economic sense. In 1860, the 6 percent of white families who owned at least twenty slaves held over half of the state's property value. Meanwhile, roughly half of the thirty thousand Georgia farmers who owned fewer than a hundred acres were slaveholders with fewer than five slaves. Though not rich when compared with their planter neighbors, these yeomen maintained a relatively secure and independent existence by concentrating first on subsistence crops and then growing smaller amounts of cotton for domestic use and the market as well. In good years, members of this sturdy yeomanry had managed to climb to higher rungs in the slaveholding hierarchy, although as slave prices rose dramatically in relation to cotton prices, this feat was increasingly hard to accomplish, and the percentage of white families who owned slaves actually declined during the late antebellum era.

GEORGIA GOES TO WAR, AND
WAR COMES TO GEORGIA

The widening gap in wealth and opportunity between slaveholders and nonslaveholders only heightened tensions as the debate over secession grew more heated. Because Georgia was centrally located within the South, its decision was absolutely crucial to the success of the disunionist movement. Not only was Georgia the second-largest state east of the Mississippi (before West Virginia became a separate state, Virginia was the largest), but it had the largest population, the most slaves, and the most slaveholders of any Deep South state. On the other hand, two-thirds of Georgia's white population were nonslaveholders. Consequently, the stakes were high and the atmosphere tense as the legislature met in the capital city of Milledgeville in mid-November 1860. If Georgia failed to secede, hopes for the creation of a separate, unified southern nation would be dimmed considerably or even extinguished altogether.

As the Milledgeville debates unfolded, the likelihood that Georgia would remain in the Union seemed real indeed, given the prominence of more moderate leaders such as Alexander Stephens (later vice president of the Confederate States of America), a friend of the newly elected Abraham Lincoln. The secessionists had some able spokesmen as well, including Henry L. Benning, who took to the podium near the end of the debate. A lawyer and judge, Benning was acting in part as a stand-in for his old college friend and longtime rival Howell Cobb. Benning considered himself intellectually superior to Cobb, and while he languished in relative obscurity, he had grown increasingly frustrated as the more politically astute Cobb rose to prominence in state and national affairs.

Although he became the namesake of Georgia's Fort Benning, as a general (nicknamed "Old Rock"), Benning fell well short of winning the recognition he desperately sought. Still, he had his one shining hour as he stood before the legislature on November 18, 1860, and made his impassioned case for secession. He raised certain legal and constitutional issues, but Benning's real focus was the future of slavery, and his "first proposition" was "that the election of Mr. Lincoln to the Presidency of the United States means the abolition of slavery as soon as the party which elected him shall acquire the power to do the deed." Benning foresaw abolition as "one of the direst evils of which the mind can conceive." He predicted that soon after any abolition decree "a war between the whites and the blacks will spontaneously break out everywhere . . . in every town, in every village, in every neighborhood, in every road . . . a war of man with man — a war of extermination." In Benning's mind, the only way to escape the "horrors of abolition" was to leave the Union: "Men of Georgia! It is our business to save ourselves. . . . And if nothing else will save us but going out of the Union, we must go out of the Union, however much we may deplore it."

The legislature ultimately approved a bill authorizing a convention to be elected by a statewide vote on January 2, 1861. This vote yielded a bare 51 percent majority vote for delegates favoring secession, and seventeen days later, the convention produced a similarly narrow vote, 166–130, in favor of secession.

Considering the slim margin by which the ordinance of secession was ratified, Georgia's "fire-eaters" exhibited remarkable bravado. A widely circulated, likely apocryphal story about fiery disunionist Robert Toombs illustrates the differences in the attitudes of white Georgians as they entered and emerged from the Civil War. With war imminent, General Toombs (Toombs was one of the Confederacy's many questionable "political" military appointments) supposedly strode down the street in his hometown of Washington. He encountered a coquettish southern belle who twirled her parasol, blinked her eyes, and demanded to know, "General Toombs, do you really think we can whip them Yankees?" The supremely confident Toombs reassured her immediately: "Why, my dear, don't you worry yo' pretty little head. We can whip them Yankees with cornstalks."

Four years later, Toombs, looking considerably less confident, had the misfortune to encounter the same female, looking not so young and feeling not so coquettish. When she spied Toombs, she accosted him straightway, reminding him, "General Toombs, you said we could whip them Yankees with cornstalks!" "Yes, my dear, I did," the quick-witted Toombs gloomily conceded, "but the sons-a-bitches wouldn't *fight* with cornstalks!"

Like other hot-headed, delusional secessionists, Toombs had helped to set the stage for a war over slavery that, in the main, those who owned no slaves would have to fight. Although it is fairly easy to discern the motives of those who insisted on secession, it is by no means certain that everyone who went off to war was marching to their tune. In fact, many who took up arms were motivated as much as anything by a simple determination to defend their homes, their communities, and their state. The young Georgia private who declared, "If I can't fight in the name of my own state, then I don't want to fight at all," may not have been typical, but he certainly was not terribly exceptional either.

The war had not long progressed before most Georgians realized that defending their state would be no quick or easy matter. Early thoughts of a speedy victory dissolved into waves of tragedy and despair as young men by the thousands lost their lives on distant, then not-so-distant, battlefields, while deprivation and a growing anxiety about survival became a way of life on the home front. In October 1862, Mrs. A. E. Moore of Fort Valley wrote Georgia's governor Joseph E. Brown, complaining that salt was $125 per sack and flour $40 per barrel. "How in the world are poor people to live?" Mrs. Moore asked. A widow with three small children who was also supporting her mother, Mrs. Moore demanded, "Must poor widows and helpless orphans be brought to suffering even for bread?"

Since Georgia's men in gray were hearing much the same thing from their loved ones, desertion soon became a major problem. Indeed, it is surprising that desertion rates were not higher. Confederate troops suffered horribly from even more severe shortages of their own, and they compounded matters as they began to strip the countryside of food, livestock, and other necessities. From Whitfield County in September 1863, John W. Cain complained that the Confederate cavalry was taking horses, killing sheep and hogs, stealing chickens, and even digging potatoes out of the ground. "All manner of depredation is committed," Cain reported to Governor Brown. When Georgia's home guard was pressed into service in defense of the state, members complained of having to leave families and crops and expressed fears of a Negro uprising. On Christmas Eve 1864, one Chattooga County citizen-soldier informed Governor Brown that his colleagues were "in no condition for fighting, for they are distressed so much on account of their families and property that they seem to care for nothing else."

If any Georgians yet had cause to doubt it, Gen. William Tecumseh Sherman's 1864 conquest of Atlanta and subsequent March to the Sea clearly taught them that war was indeed hell. Shocked that he had begun "to regard death and mangling of a couple of thousand men as a small affair," Sherman himself reported to his wife, "We have devoured the land. All the people retire before us and desolation is behind. To realize what war is, one should follow our tracks." On the road to Atlanta, a member of Sherman's party saw a young mother skinning a cow while her little daughter, obviously starving, tore at the raw carcass with her hands.

As Sherman's troops approached Atlanta, a Mariettan, Minerva McClatchey, bemoaned their uncivilized behavior: "They took everything, tore the green grapes from the vines, tramped over the garden, and destroyed everything. If this is the way they do in the daytime, what may we expect tonight?" Those in Sherman's path saw not just the destruction of property but of the social and moral fabric as well. Nancy Jett complained that several of her friends had turned to "whoring," sometimes going into the Union camps to "fetch their beaus home at night."

As the battle for Atlanta raged, B. W. Froebel described "shells . . . screaming across the sky like blazing comets" and raining down "like sulfurous hail." Even Sherman's adjutant, Henry Hitchcock, was shocked by what he described as "the grandest and most awful scene" of Atlanta as it was consumed by "huge waves of fire, roaring, blazing, furious flames."

When Sherman's columns left much of Atlanta in ashes and rubble and moved south toward Macon before turning toward Savannah, Dolly Lunt Burge recorded in her diary a visit from Yankee "demons": "To my smoke-house, my dairy, pantry, kitchen and cellar, like famished wolves they come." Beset for a month by blue-clad invaders, Mary Jones of Liberty County saw in her desperate plight the wrath of Jehovah as well as that of Sherman: "Clouds and darkness are around us. The hand of the Almighty is laid in sore judgment upon us. . . . We are a desolate and smitten people."

After reaching Savannah, Rufus Mead, a Union soldier from Connecticut, was nothing short of exultant: "We had a glorious old tramp right through the heart of the state, rioted and feasted on the country, destroyed all the RR, in short found a rich and overflowing country filled with cattle, hogs, sheep and fowls, corn, sweet potatoes, and syrup, but left a barren waste for miles on either side of the road, burnt millions of dollars of property, wasted and destroyed all the eatables we couldn't carry off and brought the war to the doors of the Georgians so effectively, I guess they will long remember the Yankees."

Mead clearly had a gift for understatement. On December 16, 1864, as Sherman prepared to make the city of Savannah a Christmas present to Pres. Abraham Lincoln, a disconsolate F. M. Hawkins pleaded with Governor Brown to do what he could to "stop the effusion of innocent blood, stay the hand of the destroying angel, open the way to negotiation and expedite peace." Blaming the conflict on the politicians who "continue to grovel in human blood for place, power and wealth," Hawkins warned that if "this fratricidal conflict" was not brought to a speedy end, "ruin, fearful ruin, to our whole people will be the inevitable result."

Peace brought no immediate relief, however. In May 1865 Eliza Frances Andrews noted in her journal, "Our own disbanded armies, ragged, starving, hopeless, reckless, are roaming about without order or leaders, making their way to their far off homes as best they can. Everything is in a state of disorganization and tumult. We have no currency, no law save the primitive code that might makes right. We are in a transition state from war to subjugation. The suspense and anxiety in which we live are terrible."

Eliza Frances Andrews no doubt reflected the gloomy outlook of the majority of white Georgians as military hostilities ceased. Black Georgians enjoyed an entirely different perspective, however. Theirs was a transition from subjugation toward what they hoped would be a far better life, one in which they would enjoy the benefits of personal freedom, political legitimacy, and economic opportunity. Even with the war in its early stages, slaveowners had noted a pattern of independence and insolence among their slaves that grew only more pronounced as the conflict progressed. When Union troops drew near, escapes became more common, especially after Sherman's troops began making their way to Atlanta. Escaping slaves made their way to Union lines, many of them to enlist in the fight for freedom. More than thirty-five hundred Georgia bondsmen served the Union cause. Incredible as it seems in hindsight, most white Georgians expressed great surprise and dismay that their slaves would desert them and flee to the Yankees.

The reaction of Mrs. H. J. Wayne, recorded as Sherman approached Savannah, was fairly typical: "We left Savannah in a very great hurry as the Yankees had cut every road and were in force only three miles from the city. . . . Every one of my negroes left me the morning I left which was a great shock as they did not even appear unwilling to come with me but they are so artful and have such an idea of freedom. [O]nly three or four families left before me and all of their servants ran away but mine have always appeared so faithful that I had too much confidence in them."

Upon claiming their freedom, black Georgians set out immediately to reunite their families and settle down in a stable home environment. Georgia planter David Barrow conceded that it "was commonly thought that the Negroes, when freed, would care very little for their children, and would let them die for want of attention, but experience . . . proved this surmise unfounded."

Meanwhile, for the cruel master who had so brutally whipped William Colbert's brother January, there was no family left to reunite: "De massa had three boys to go to war, but dere wuzn't one to come home. All the chillun he had wuz killed. Massa, he los' all his money and de house soon begin droppin' away to nothin'. Us niggers one by one lef' de ole place and de las' time I seed de home plantation I wuz a standin' on a hill. I looked back on it for de las' time through a patch of scrub pines and it look' so lonely. Dere warn't but one person in sight, de massa. He was a-settin' in a wicker chair in de yard lookin' out ober a small field of cotton and cawn. Dere wuz fo' crosses in de graveyard in de side lawn where he wuz a-settin'. De fo'th one wuz his wife."

Colbert's recollections of his master's personal and financial devastation might serve as a metaphor for most of the white population in a state that had lost some forty thousand men to the war and seen its economy all but destroyed as well. Georgia had produced more than seven hundred thousand bales of cotton in 1860; the 1865 crop was closer to fifty thousand.

RECONSTRUCTION: ADVANCE AND RETREAT

While black Georgians had set about even before the war's end to build a new world for themselves, white Georgians undertook, insofar as possible, to recreate the old world that had been destroyed by the war they fought to save it. Under the leadership of provisional governor James Johnson, white politicians forged a postwar constitution acknowledging the supremacy of the U.S. Constitution and the abolition of slavery. It also repealed the ordinance of secession and repudiated the state's war debt (in excess of eighteen million dollars). The new constitution extended the vote to only "free white male citizens," however, and the legislature soon passed a number of vagrancy and antienticement statutes designed to restore white control of black labor. The legislature authorized public schools for whites without mentioning blacks, who were also excluded from service on juries. Both houses of the legislature emphatically rejected the Fourteenth Amendment, which aimed to extend the rights of citizenship and due process to blacks. The legislators also elected former Confederate vice president Alexander H. Stephens and former Confederate senator Herschel V. Johnson to the U.S. Senate.

Northern critics seized on Stephens's election in particular as evidence that southern whites had not truly accepted the outcome and consequences of the war. Thus, the legislature's actions, along with the more extreme measures taken by some of Georgia's southern neighbors, helped to strengthen the hand of the radical Republicans in Congress and, in turn, to bring on Military Reconstruction in the spring of 1867. After federal troops oversaw the registration of black voters, a new constitutional convention accorded blacks the rights of citizenship and the vote and the ostensible guarantee of equal protection of the law. Republican strength in Georgia drew primarily on a tenuous coalition of former Unionist whites, who were not in the main particularly enamored of the notion of black equality, and the newly enfranchised freedmen. Hence the convention, in a move that proved to be significant indeed, shied away from a straightforward guarantee of the right of blacks to hold office after Democratic delegates threatened to bolt the convention if such a provision were approved. The delegates elected as well to retain the highly exclusionary poll tax as a prerequisite for voting.

In April 1868, the special elections to ratify the constitution and fill the state's elective offices foretold the brief and turbulent future of Congressional Reconstruction in Georgia. White Republicans courted white votes with assurances that blacks could not hold office in Georgia even as fifty black Republicans sought legislative seats. Meanwhile, Georgia Democrats pursued a strategy that was part politics and part guerrilla warfare. Former Confederate general John B. Gordon, a Yankee-inflicted scar adorning his cheek, was the Democratic nominee for governor and the acknowledged head of the Ku Klux Klan in the state. With the Klan functioning as the terrorist arm of the Democratic Party and Democratic leaders like former Confederate senator Benjamin H. Hill insisting that whites who voted Republican "should be driven from the white race, as Lucifer was driven from heaven into a social Hell," the Democrats put up a strong late effort. Nonetheless, Republican Rufus Bullock captured the governorship, thanks in no small measure to the support of black voters, who also managed to elect thirty-two of their own to the legislature as the Republicans secured a solid majority in both houses.

The early days of Bullock's administration seemed full of promise. The legislature ratified the Fourteenth Amendment, and the governor dismissed the issue of white supremacy with the observation that "all civilized men are citizens." (It would be more than a hundred years before a Georgia governor again took such a moderate position on race.) Bullock promised "peace and plenty," but the Republicans in the legislature were divided and undisciplined. The Democrats succeeded in ousting all but four of the thirty-two blacks elected to the legislature on the grounds that the state's constitution did not provide for black officeholding. (The favored four were mulattos and were accorded the curious status of "honorary whites.")

The regular general election in November 1868 featured all manner of violence and intimidation, including the "Camilla Massacre" in which at least nine black Republicans were killed. Although blacks sometimes gave as good as they got, in the wake of the sweeping Democratic victory, Republican officeholders were at severe personal risk of injury or death whenever they appeared in public. With lawlessness and disorder continuing, Georgia was again placed under Military Reconstruction. Black legislators returned to claim their seats in December 1869, and twenty-two conservative Democrats were disqualified by a military board. The legislature again ratified the Fourteenth Amendment and the Fifteenth Amendment as well and also authorized the creation of a segregated but ostensibly "equal" system of common schools.

Again, however, this renewed effort at Reconstruction was over shortly after it began. The Republicans had never succeeded in putting together a permanent working majority in the state, and the Democrats claimed commanding control of the legislature in another violence- and intimidation-marred election in December 1870. After trying unsuccessfully to have Georgia put under military rule once more, Governor Bullock fled the state to avoid impeachment. When Democrat James M. Smith won a special election to succeed Bullock in 1871, Georgia was effectively "redeemed" from Radical Reconstruction. The following year, Smith won the regular gubernatorial election, and in contrast to four years earlier when thirty-two black legislators were selected by the voters, only four won office in 1872. The poll tax subsequently kept blacks away from the polls in large numbers as did the continuing threat of violence, although W. H. Rogers, the last Reconstruction-era black legislator, remained in office until 1907.

The ups and downs of Reconstruction for black Georgians manifested themselves with particular clarity in coastal McIntosh County. A New Jersey native who had served as a leader in the so-called "Sea Island experiment" in black self-sufficiency ordained by General Sherman during the war, Tunis G. Campbell represented McIntosh County as a state senator and served as a justice of the peace. Campbell insisted on equal representation of blacks on juries and otherwise championed their rights to the point of making himself a source of "constant annoyance" to local whites. In 1873 the legislature ousted Campbell from his seat in that body and appointed a board of commissioners to take over local government in McIntosh County. At age sixty-three, Campbell was sentenced, on trumped-up charges of improper conduct, to a year at hard labor, a year that he served, ironically enough, as a leased laborer on a plantation.

Meanwhile, Governor Smith urged blacks to "get down to honest hard work," and the legislature set about to see that this admonition was followed, passing a host of statutes designed to restrict the mobility and economic rights and opportunities of the freedmen. Historian Eric Foner cited Georgia's example as "the most comprehensive effort to undo Reconstruction," and Smith offered a suitable benediction for this effort (also revealing the motivation behind it) when he remarked that, with Reconstruction out of the way, whites could "hold inviolate every law of the United States and still so legislate upon our labor system as to retain old plantation system."

LIFE AND LABOR IN POSTBELLUM GEORGIA

It was one thing to retain the old system but quite another to make it profitable again. In 1860 the average white male Georgian had a net worth of about $4,000, approximately twice as much as the average nonsouthern male. By 1870 this figure had plummeted to about $1,400 (in 1860 dollars), far less than half the earlier figure and now less than three-fourths of the nonsouthern average. Economic problems of all sorts abounded. The loss of the slave labor force dealt a severe blow to cotton production. The evaporation of approximately $416 million in slave capital and, just as important, collateral, also left Georgia agriculture in dire financial circumstances. These circumstances seemed bleaker still in light of a noticeable slowdown in the growth of world cotton demand, manifested in a general decline in cotton prices, which stood at eleven cents per pound in the mid-1870s and six cents per pound twenty years later.

While the South was out of the Union, the national banking system had been reorganized without input from the representatives of southern agriculture. As a result, banks were, to say the least, scarce in the land of cotton. In 1894 at least 123 of Georgia's counties had no banks of any sort. With such banks as there were refusing to make loans when land was the only available collateral, all but the most affluent of Georgia's farmers turned to merchants and large planters for credit. They secured this credit by mortgaging not their land but their crops. (Lenders believed quite rightly that cotton could be converted to cash more readily than could land.) Hence, under the so-called crop-lien system, farmers found themselves mortgaging an unplanted crop at an unspecified rate of interest for a loan of undetermined value. The deficiencies of such a credit scheme were obvious enough. For a typical farmer, the question was not whether he built up a substantial debt at a huge rate of interest but simply to whom (planter or merchant) he ultimately owed that debt.

The generally declining growth of world cotton demand throughout the late nineteenth century suggested that cotton growers should diversify their operations, but the crop-lien system required the cultivation of a cash crop to secure the lien, and no viable crop promised a better cash return than cotton. By way of example, despite falling cotton prices, the cash yield per acre for corn between 1866 and 1900 was less than half that for cotton. As a result, Georgia farmers had little choice but to grow more and more of a crop for which they could expect to be compensated less and less. Since the size of the lien often exceeded the market value of the crop, recurrent, mounting, crippling, and ultimately destructive debt was a way of life among Georgia farmers. Through forced sales and foreclosures, anyone who supplied credit soon acquired land in sizable quantities. Meanwhile, on the other side of the ledger, many families who had owned their land for generations eventually found themselves either turned off it or farming it as tenants under the onerous lien system. By 1880, tenants accounted for one-third of Georgia's farmers.

Although thousands of white farmers would soon be tumbling down the agricultural ladder to join them, in the first decades after Reconstruction, the majority of Georgia's tenants were black. Having refused to work for their former masters in closely supervised gangs (an arrangement they found all too reminiscent of slavery), large numbers of Georgia's landless freedpeople had actually chosen tenancy as their best available option. Initially, at least, many blacks managed to make some progress by contracting to work designated portions of larger land holdings for a share of the crop in exchange for varying kinds of support, ranging from housing, food, clothing, and other necessities to seed, fertilizer, and the use of mules and implements. Yet where blacks had initially entered into sharecropping arrangements as more or less autonomous "partners in the crop," as time passed whites succeeded in reshaping the sharecropping system to their own advantage. Through a combination of coercion, custom, and law, they gradually gained more and more control over the sharecroppers' lives, destroying their cherished autonomy and replacing it with close supervision of every phase of cotton production. At the same time, through a series of laws and questionable legal rulings, these planters also succeeded in gaining control over the marketing of the crop so that the cropper generally had little or no say about where and when the cotton would be sold or at what price. On "settlement" day, croppers lined up at the plantation commissaries or the farmers' porches to learn how they had fared (or more accurately how the landlord said they had fared). Even if the croppers received an honest settlement, the odds against them were bad enough, since the effective interest rate charged by merchants during the 1880s hovered around the 60 percent mark. All too often, however, the black cropper had to contend with being "counted out" by the white man. Not surprisingly, Georgia blacks often repeated a folk saying common throughout the South:

> An ought's an ought
> And a figger's a figger.
> All for the white man
> And none for the nigger.

Not all blacks accepted this somber reality, but when they did not, they usually found that the price of demanding fair treatment was high indeed. Martin Luther King Sr. recounted an incident from his childhood that occurred in 1911 but might have taken place at almost any point during the last years of the nineteenth century or the first half of the twentieth. As a twelve-year-old boy, "Daddy" King had gone along when his own father went to "settle" with the landlord. King's father warned him repeatedly to keep his mouth shut, but when the landlord ignored the money due his father for his cotton seed, the young man was unable to contain himself, and he blurted out, "But, Poppa . . . ain't nothin' been said about the cotton seed." The landlord turned "beet red" and threatened to kick young Martin's "little butt."

The elder King's response astonished not only the landlord, but the crowd of white onlookers as well: "Don't nobody touch my boy, Mr. Graves. Anything need to be done to him, I'll take care of it." The furious landlord moved nearer to his tenant, demanding to know, "Who the hell you think you're talking to, Nigger?" A loose circle formed around the two men, but the tension was broken when young King again spoke up, reminding his father, "Ain't nothin' been said yet 'bout the cotton seed!" The tension erupted into laughter as the white men howled about the temerity of the young black boy, and they were soon urging the landlord to pay Martin's father what he owed him. The elder King received his money, far more than his son believed even existed, but he also received a chilling assurance from the landlord: "Boy, . . . I'm gon' see from now on that you get everything you got comin'. I'm gon' see to it personally."

Young Martin failed to grasp the significance of these remarks, and he was hurt and confused by his father's anger at him as the two rode home. At sunrise the next morning, he began to understand. The landlord and some of his men had come and taken the mule and some of the implements upon which his father had been paying and ordered him to be off the place by sundown. The family packed their belongings into the wagon, but since the landlord had taken the mule, they had to push the wagon toward town. Years later, King recalled that experience: "The look on Papa's face told me we were in trouble. He was in pain. For getting only what was right, what was due him, he now had to get off the shares he'd been working. His family was without a home. What did being 'right' mean, I wondered, if you had to suffer so much for it?"

In many ways, Georgia's white tenants fared little better. Though they were less vulnerable to physical violence and coercion and could therefore demand "fairness" from their landlords with less risk, they found themselves in a system and a situation that seemed to them intrinsically unfair. In the antebellum era, Georgia's white yeomen had been able to enjoy a relatively independent existence on their own land, practicing what economists later called "safety-first" agriculture by growing their own foodstuffs (any surplus of which might be bartered for items not produced by the farmer) and then devoting whatever time or acreage that remained to cotton, the proceeds of which might be accumulated to purchase slaves and more land. The end of slavery and the rise of the crop-lien system brought about the demise of safety-first agriculture as merchants offered credit for cash crops only, forcing yeomen to grow more cotton and, increasingly, to become purchasers of some of the foodstuffs they had formerly produced. Efforts to fence in the open range further threatened their self-sufficiency by restricting their ability to raise livestock and allow it to graze in the open, uncultivated woodlands and fields. The long-term result, readily discernible even in the short term, was that ever-increasing numbers of small-scale white farmers found themselves tumbling headlong into dependency, debt, and tenancy with little hope of reversing their own fortunes or of creating a better life for their children. If Georgia's white farmers had ever approximated Thomas Jefferson's heroic ideal of the sturdy, independent, salt-of-the-earth agrarian, by the end of the nineteenth century any such resemblance was scant indeed.

Census reports (which defined each tenant tract as a "farm") documented this disturbing trend. In 1880 two-thirds of Georgia's farms had been tilled by their owners; by 1920 two-thirds were worked by tenants. Because the amount of cropland available was effectively finite, as the ranks of tenants swelled, the size of the tracts on which they depended for a living shrank proportionately. By 1920 average farm size had fallen to less than 20 percent of what it had been in 1860.

Those caught up in this destructive downward spiral could expect little sympathy from the state's reigning "Bourbon Triumvirate," consisting of former Confederate governor Joseph E. Brown and former Confederate generals John B. Gordon and A. H. Colquitt. The three had helped to overthrow Reconstruction in 1870 and 1871, and for the next eighteen years, they would dominate both the state's governorship and its seats in the U.S. Senate. Heavily involved in railroad speculation, coal mining (with convict labor in the cases of Brown and Gordon), and other industrial and business ventures, they consistently pursued their personal economic and political interests with solicitous regard for the concerns of Georgia's powerful industrialists and large planters, while barely giving even lip service to the needs of its beleaguered small farmers.

AGRARIAN UPRISING

Having little to lose but their misery, Georgia's farmers rose in political revolt at the end of the nineteenth century. The most dynamic figure in the agrarian uprising in Georgia was Thomas E. Watson. Born into a once-prosperous plantation family fallen on hard times, Watson worked first as a teacher, then became a successful attorney, and ultimately reclaimed his family's plantation holdings in McDuffie County, near Thomson. He won a state legislative seat in 1882 and went to Congress in 1890. Watson became an eloquent spokesman for the Populist Party, which had grown primarily out of the Farmers' Alliance, an organization that spread from Texas into Georgia. The Alliance movement stressed cooperative action, and its Georgia branch was notably successful in establishing a state cooperative farm exchange in Atlanta that bought fertilizer and other supplies in high volume and made them available at lower prices than would otherwise have been possible. The Alliance also sought the assistance of Washington, however, championing the "subtreasury plan" whereby farmers would store their crops at strategically located warehouses and receive loans of up to 80 percent of their value. Hoping to relieve further the credit shortage that had proven so disadvantageous to most farmers, the Alliance spokesmen also called on the federal government to expand the money supply by printing new currency to fund the loans issued through the subtreasury plan. Not surprisingly, most conservatives and even many moderates considered both the expansion of the currency and the subtreasury plan unspeakably radical.

To many white Georgians, however, the most radical aspect of the

Farmers' Alliance–Populist threat was not economic but racial, for the agrarian insurgency reached out to blacks and called on them to join in a counterattack on the forces that seemed bent on impoverishing and humiliating all but the wealthiest and most powerful farmers of both races. Since the end of Reconstruction, conservative and relatively affluent white Democrats had managed to maintain their political dominance by bombarding lower-class whites with the threat of the "negro domination" that was certain to result if whites did not remain politically unified. Recasting the issue in terms of simple self-interest, Watson argued that "the accident of color can make no difference in the interest of farmers, croppers, and laborers."

His efforts won Watson all manner of vituperation as well as threats of physical abuse and even death. He and his followers also faced the reality of economic intimidation by planters, merchants, and bankers. Though they made no grassroots appeals to black voters, white conservatives worked with key black leaders to claim a large share of the black vote. Beyond that, there was the simple matter of fraud. Watson lost his bid for reelection to Congress in 1892, primarily because of his poor showing in Richmond County, where ten thousand voters somehow managed to cast more than twelve thousand ballots. Watson went on, however, to achieve national status as a Populist leader, gaining the party's nomination for vice president in 1896.

Even as Watson received this recognition, however, at the national level the Populists were signing their own death warrant. After the Democrats had reached out to them by writing into their platform the Populists' call for the free and unlimited coinage of silver and nominating free-silver advocate William Jennings Bryan for president, Populists took the bait and endorsed Bryan before naming Watson as their vice presidential choice. Watson and the Populists were quickly lost in the shuffle as conservative Democrats left the party in droves, and Bryan went down to a predictably devastating defeat.

The demise of the Populists at the national level said much about the American political system, but their ill-fated assault on the status quo was perhaps even more revealing about the intertwined social and political realities of life in turn-of-the-century Georgia. Certainly, the Populist debacle underscored the strength of the Democratic Party in the state, but more important, it demonstrated that the color line was still the bottom line in Georgia politics. A frustrated Watson complained, "You might beseech a Southern white tenant to listen to you upon questions of finance, taxation, and transportation; you might demonstrate with mathematical precision that herein lay his way out of poverty into comfort; you might have him 'almost persuaded' to the truth, but if the merchant who furnished his farm supplies (at tremendous usury) or the town politician (who never spoke to him excepting at election times) came along and cried 'Negro rule!' the entire fabric of reason and common sense which you had patiently constructed would fall, and the poor tenant would joyously hug the chains of an actual wretchedness rather than do any experimenting on a question of mere sentiment."

The defeat of the Populist insurgents shut the door on prospects for a color-blind political alliance. It also paved the way for a comprehensive effort by the state's conservative Democratic leadership to provide long-term solutions for the state's racial and economic problems once and for all. Led by Henry Woodfin Grady, the "New South" crusade sought to promote prosperity through economic diversification, especially the rapid expansion of industry. Grady, who was born to comfortable circumstances in Athens, went on to become the editor of the *Atlanta Constitution*, in which capacity he frequently served both as the mouthpiece for the Bourbon Triumvirate and as Atlanta's biggest booster. He insisted that the only hope for Georgia and the South at large to throw off the long-term economic subjection that was even more insidious than the unpleasant interim of Reconstruction lay in industrial development: "The farmers may farm as wisely as they please, but as long as we manufacture nothing and rely on the shops and mills and factories of other sections for everything we use, our section must remain dependent and poor."

To illustrate his point, Grady recounted on numerous occasions an apocryphal account of a funeral he claimed to have attended in Pickens County, Georgia: "They buried him in the midst of a marble quarry: they cut through solid marble to make his grave; and yet a little tombstone they put above him was from Vermont. They buried him in the heart of a pine forest, and yet the pine coffin was imported from Cincinnati. They buried him within touch of an iron mine, and yet the nails in his coffin and the iron in the shovel that dug his grave were imported from Pittsburg [*sic*]. They buried him by the side of the best sheep-grazing country on earth, and yet the wool in the coffin bands and the coffin bands themselves were brought from the North. The South didn't furnish a thing on earth for that funeral but the corpse and the hole in the ground."

To remedy this deplorable situation, Grady urged his fellow Georgians to stop feeling sorry for themselves and get about the business of rebuilding their state. Grady realized, however, that, given the scarcity of capital in the state and region, this rebuilding process would go nowhere without the financial assistance of northern investors. Hence, he preached the gospel of sectional reconciliation: "Every dollar of Northern money reinvested in the South gives us a new friend in that section."

The clean-living, baby-faced Grady quickly established himself as the South's most eloquent spokesman for economic change. Being too young to have taken up arms against the Union in 1861 made Grady even more respectable in northern eyes, and when the New England Society of New York decided to seek a southerner to speak at its 1886 banquet at Delmonico's in New York City, he was a logical choice. Still in his midthirties at the time, Grady did not disappoint, despite having to share the platform with one William Tecumseh Sherman in whose honor the band played "Marching through Georgia," which was, to say the least, hardly one of Grady's favorite tunes.

As the audience, 360 primarily conservative businessmen seeking assurances that their investment capital would be safe in the South, leaned forward, Grady showcased his renowned talent for oratory — and hyperbole: "There was a South of slavery and secession — that South is dead. There is a South of union and freedom — that South, thank God, is living, breathing, growing every hour." To put his audience at ease, Grady paid tribute to Abraham Lincoln, and though he chided him for being slightly careless with fire, Grady all but thanked Sherman for burning Atlanta, from whose ashes had risen a "brave and beautiful city" where "somehow or other we have caught the sunshine in the bricks and mortar of our homes, and have builded therein not one ignoble prejudice or memory."

To say that Grady "laid it on thick" would be to do him a grave injustice. His portrait of the homecoming of a "typical" Confederate veteran, "ragged, half-starved, heavy hearted, enfeebled by want and wounds," is but one example: "What does he find when he reaches the home he left so prosperous and beautiful? He finds his house in ruins, his farm devastated, his slaves free, his stock killed, his barns empty, his trade destroyed, his money worthless, his social system swept away, his people without law or legal status, his comrades slain and the burdens of others heavy on his shoulders. Crushed by defeat, his very traditions are gone."

To illustrate the courage and resourcefulness of such ex-Confederates, Grady turned to the example of his "business partner," who found himself not only without home or money but, if Grady is to be believed, without pants as well. After his wife cut up an old woolen dress to make him some britches, Grady's partner went out and made himself rich, parlaying a five-dollar gold piece given him by his father into a net wealth of $250,000.

With his audience by now alternately cheering and weeping, Grady made his move on their pocketbooks, urging well-heeled investors to "come on down" (quotes mine): "We have learned that one Northern immigrant is worth fifty foreigners and have smoothed the path to southward, wiped out the place where Mason and Dixon's line used to be. We have fallen in love with work! We know that we have achieved in peace a fuller independence for the South than that which our fathers sought to win by their swords."

JIM CROW'S GEORGIA

The picture of harmony, unity, stability, and progress painted by Grady was more than slightly at odds with the facts. Although Grady insisted that "the relations of the Southern people with the Negro are close and cordial," Georgia averaged a lynching a month in the 1890s and led the nation in lynchings between 1899 (when twenty-seven were recorded) and 1918. Over the half century between 1882 and 1930, 95 percent of the victims of lynching in Georgia were black. Of the 435 blacks who were lynched in Georgia during this period, 86 percent were killed in either the Cotton Belt or South Georgia, the areas where the black population was most concentrated. These regions were also home to the state's largest plantations, whose owners were acutely sensitive to the need to retain control of their black labor supply and often nervous well past the point of paranoia about their safety as they surveyed the masses of blacks swirling around the town squares on Saturday afternoons. For whites in these areas, a lynching represented an explosive release, partly of hatred, but perhaps even more so of fear. The first reason commonly given for lynching a black person was an alleged physical attack, fatal or not, on a white person; the second, an alleged sexual assault on a white woman. Whatever their ostensible motivation, in the long run, it mattered little to the mob whether the victim was guilty as accused. A hanging or a burning, with all the mutilations and horrors that might accompany it, served notice to local blacks that the consequences of violating the delicate etiquette of white supremacy were severe indeed.

Rather than spontaneous explosions of mob violence, lynchings were more like rituals aimed at reaffirming white supremacy and reminding blacks that any wrong move might bring swift and horrible retribution. In 1899 a crowd of two thousand celebrated a Sabbath afternoon by witnessing the torture, burning, and mutilation of a black victim in

Newnan. Accommodating railroad officials had provided special excursion trains for Atlantans, who made the trip down into a full-blown and almost festive outing.

Coupled with what surely seemed at times like nothing less than a reign of lawlessness and terror against blacks came a move to legalize and institutionalize a rigid system of racial separation in Georgia. (In Georgia, as elsewhere, these statutes were soon known as "Jim Crow" laws, drawing their identity from a popular blackface minstrel character.) When segregation finally came under fire in the mid-1950s, its assailants identified it with the intense racism associated with the plantation and the southern countryside in general. In reality, however, segregation was an urban phenomenon, one rendered necessary in the eyes of whites by the destruction of slavery and the increased movement of the black population into the city.

In the years surrounding the turn of the century, Georgia municipalities produced a plethora of ordinances mandating separate seating, facilities, and accommodations in a host of settings from street cars to prison camps to taverns. In settings such as libraries or swimming pools, where segregation was unfeasible, blacks were simply excluded. The color line ran everywhere. Stories about separate Bibles for swearing in witnesses of different races are not exaggerations, nor is it hard to believe that when a black college president saw a white woman tumbling down the steps at the train station in Atlanta, he instantly suppressed his impulse to reach out and break her fall and simply allowed her to take a nasty spill. Black audiences thought this a laughable example of the stupidity of Jim Crow customs, but a great many southern whites, perhaps even the injured woman herself, might well have deemed the man's behavior entirely appropriate under the circumstances.

In many cases, Jim Crow laws merely codified well-established practices, but even so, some historians have argued, the emergence of segregation by law rather than custom made the general inclination to discriminate considerably stronger and more respectable. In Atlanta and some other Georgia cities, however, measures such as those requiring racial separation on streetcars and local trains, both of which depended significantly on black passengers for revenue, were slow to go into effect and then often indifferently observed. In some cities, blacks protested the new ordinances and tried to initiate boycotts of Jim Crow street-cars, but in the racial climate of turn-of-the-century Georgia, adopting too aggressive a posture was likely to prove fatal. Georgia blacks had little choice but to accede, for the time being, at least, to the new order by retreating from any sort of social contact with whites and establishing and strengthening their own economic, social, civic, and religious institutions. This network of churches, clubs, lodges, and businesses provided a strong sense of community that sustained black Georgians through three-quarters of a century of life under Jim Crow, and it remains a vital part of their cultural identity even today.

As Georgia whites took steps to institutionalize their control over social interaction with blacks, they moved simultaneously to neutralize them politically. The Constitution of 1877 required would-be voters to pay a poll tax in order to cast a ballot in Georgia. In 1900 the Georgia Democratic Party established a statewide primary system as a means of nominating its candidates for office. The primary was supposed to be more democratic than the old system of selecting candidates at conventions, but the new statewide primary was open only to Georgians with white skin. Since the Democrats were firmly established as the dominant political party in the state, winning the Democratic primary was tantamount to winning the general election and, therefore, exclusion from the white primary meant exclusion from the only election in Georgia that really mattered.

Although the poll tax and white primary seemed to provide formidable barriers to black political participation, Georgia's Democratic leadership was still not satisfied. Consequently, the need for further restrictions on black voting became the central issue in a 1906 gubernatorial campaign that unleashed the horrible potential of white racial passions. With the Atlanta papers bombarding readers with stories of atrocities committed by blacks, lynchings and other abuses were rampant, and a few days after the election a bloody four-day race riot swept across Atlanta.

In 1908 Democratic leaders pushed through a constitutional amendment requiring potential registrants to pass a literacy test. As an apparent concession to whites who could not meet the literacy requirement, the amendment offered exemptions to veterans or descendants of veterans, to those who owned property of a certain value, or to those who were of "good character." These exemptions were available, however, only to those who had paid their poll taxes. To be sure, registrars judged literacy on a sliding scale according to color, and a black physician or teacher who showed the temerity to attempt to register was likely to be found illiterate by a registrar who might well have only a few years of formal schooling himself, while a truly illiterate white might "pass" the test with ease. For many whites, however, the very act of taking the test amounted to exposing their illiteracy even if their skin color largely guaranteed that they would be allowed to vote. By the same token, although whites seemed to have a variety of routes by which to circumvent the literacy requirement, to choose any of them was to admit to illiteracy, and such an act was singularly unappealing to the masses of poor but proud white Georgians. Hence, despite their ostensible purpose of disfranchising only black Georgians, by the second decade of the twentieth century, the cumulative effect of the poll tax, white primary, and literacy test was that practically all blacks and a great many lower-class whites were no longer casting ballots in Georgia. In fact, between 1920 and 1944, no election attracted as much as a quarter of the state's adult population, and only rarely did more than one-third of the potential white electorate show up. When it came to voting in Georgia, Numan V. Bartley observed, "the poor, the black, and the unschooled need not apply."

Although the advocates of disfranchisement had sold it as a means of strengthening white supremacy, its specific result was to determine as well, for decades to come, exactly which whites would actually reign supreme. More specifically, disfranchisement was a movement by, of, and for the Democratic Party. The removal of the bottom one-third of the potential electorate provided powerful insurance against a renewal of the Populist or Republican challenge. In the wake of disfranchisement, Georgia became and remained for more than half a century a solidly Democratic state, its political system functioning overwhelmingly to the benefit of a limited segment of the population and effectively insulated from any challenge by those whose interests it excluded.

The tripartite system of political neutralization, legalized discrimination, and extralegal coercion and terrorism amounted to white Georgia's "final solution" to the "race question." As early as 1885, Henry Grady had been telling all who would listen that "nowhere on earth is there kindlier feeling, closer sympathy, or less friction between two classes of society than between the whites and the blacks of the South today."

Ten years later, with racial tensions running high and the outlook for black progress as dim as it had been since the Reconstruction era, black educator and spokesman Booker T. Washington was invited to speak at the opening session of the Cotton States Exposition in Atlanta. Intended to showcase the South's progress, the exposition had a target audience consisting primarily of the investors and entrepreneurs that Grady and his disciples had been wooing so ardently. Ironically, exposition organizers drew criticism from local whites, both for their decision to have a special building for exhibits featuring black accomplishments and for their decision to allow Washington to speak, while many Atlanta blacks boycotted the extravaganza in protest of the strict policies of segregation that governed the affair.

Introduced as "a great Southern educator" and a "representative of Negro enterprise and Negro civilization," Washington began his speech under the glare of a broiling late afternoon sun. Putting his white audience at ease, Washington assured them: "The wisest among my race understand that the agitation of questions of social equality is the extremest folly." In the most famous passage from the speech, he reasoned that "in all things that are purely social, we can be as separate as the fingers, yet one as the hand in all things essential to mutual progress."

Washington asked only for fairness and cooperation from whites, assuring them that by providing reasonable economic and educational opportunities for blacks, whites "can be sure in the future, as in the past, that you and your families will be surrounded by the most patient, faithful, law-abiding, and unresentful people that the world has seen."

A New York City journalist announced that no event since Henry Grady's speech at Delmonico's in 1886 had demonstrated "so profoundly the spirit of the New South." The comparison between Washington and Grady was apt enough. Not only were the language and tone used by each man almost eerily similar, but both presented what historian Paul Gaston called "the strange mixture of wishful thinking and calculated opportunism that gave to the myth of the New South its singular force." Like Grady, Washington sought the assistance of northern financiers — "Christlike philanthropists," as he liked to call them — and also like Grady, he felt the need to assure southern whites that his efforts posed no threat to the "southern way of life."

GEORGIA: WHERE TWO WORLDS COLLIDE

It was fitting that Washington gave his famous speech in Georgia, for in no other southern state did evidence of a progressive spirit and a disposition toward primitive behavior appear in such startling juxtaposition. As the outspoken black leader W. E. B. Du Bois put it, "Georgia connotes to most men national supremacy in cotton and lynching, southern supremacy in finance and industry and the Ku Klux Klan." Attending a picnic in 1896, a Georgia youth paid a nickel to hear his very first phonograph recording. At first, an excited Mell Barrett thought he was hearing a convention or some other meeting. Then young Barrett heard a voice say, "All right, men, bring them out. Let's hear what they have to say," and he listened with growing horror as two men confessed to a rape and began to beg for mercy. Barrett then heard, "the sounds of shuffling feet, swearing men, rattle of chains, falling wood, brush, and fagots, then a voice — shrill, strident, angry, called out, 'Who will apply the torch?' 'I will,' came a chorus of high-pitched, angry voices." Barrett heard the "crackle of flames" and then the victims asking God to forgive those who were putting them to death. Finally, only the sounds of the flames remained.

Barrett described his reaction: "My eyes and mouth were dry. I tried to wet my lips, but my tongue, too, was parched. Perspiration dripped from my hands. I stood immobile, unable to move."

When the man next in line asked Barrett, "What's the matter, Son — sick?" the man in charge of the concession — "sensing what my trouble was" — hastily surmised, "Too much cake, too much lemonade. You know how boys are at a picnic."

No prominent figure better personified the contradictions that abounded in turn-of-the-century Georgia than Rebecca Lattimer Felton, the state's foremost feminist and leading reform advocate. Born into a well-to-do plantation family and married to a wealthy planter-politician, Felton attached herself to a host of causes. She condemned the convict-lease system because it exposed female convicts to sexual abuse by guards and fellow prisoners. On the matter of prohibition, Felton was as dry as they came, pointing out that "if it is morally wrong to kill one's neighbor by the bullet, it is morally wrong to kill him by the grogshop." Like many of her cohorts, Felton moved from crusading against the saloon to championing women's suffrage. In fact, she joined the two causes, pointing out that an all-male electorate had failed to support candidates who favored prohibition. Felton was not much for pulling punches. Some of her statements seemed to anticipate the most aggressive of today's feminist rhetoric: "The marriage business is a lottery. You can draw a prize, but you are more apt to draw a blank." She also told a no-doubt-shocked group of state senators that many married women in Georgia "are only permitted to live, wait on their masters, bear children, and . . . are really serfs, or common treadmill slaves in the homes where they exist until they die." When some Georgia women prominent in the United Daughters of the Confederacy spoke out in defense of "the manhood of the South," she retorted that "if they prefer to hug their chains, I have no sort of objection."

Despite Felton's strong stand, Georgia was the first state to reject the Nineteenth Amendment. Still, she spoke out for equal pay for women who performed the same jobs as men and compulsory education for rural white women. Felton wrote books, articles, and newspaper columns and spoke at numerous public gatherings. In 1922, at age eighty-seven, she became the first woman to serve in the U.S. Senate when she was appointed to fill the seat vacated by the death of Tom Watson.

As a feminist, Felton seemed well ahead of her time, and in many ways, she was. In others, however, she was clearly a product of the established order in Georgia. This was most obvious in her advocacy of lynching. As with her condemnation of the convict-lease system, Felton's views on lynching derived from what she viewed as a threat to white women, in this case the supposed danger of rape by black men. When it came to conjuring up lurid visions of lustful black males assaulting virginal white maidens, Felton could easily equal any of the South's most virulently racist demagogues: "If it requires lynching to protect women's dearest possession from raving, drunken human beasts, then I say lynch a thousand negroes a week if necessary." Felton was so adamant on this point that it became almost suicidal to cross her. When a prominent Nashville clergyman challenged her views as unrepresentative, Felton denounced him as a "slick-haired, slick-tongued Pecksniffing blatherskite" and proceeded to taunt and malign him thereafter in her columns and other communications. In 1902 when Andrew Sledd, a young professor at Emory College, wrote an article in the *Atlantic Monthly* calling for an end to lynching and a calmer approach to discussing race relations, Felton led a campaign of harassment and intimidation that encouraged the young professor to resign from Emory and leave the state.

Felton's rabid support of lynching was more disappointing because she seemed very "progressive" in many of her views on women's rights.

In reality, however, Felton's pronouncements on lynching almost paled beside those of Tom Watson, the bitterly disillusioned former Populist, who once had not only condemned the practice of lynching but preached a gospel of racial unity. By the turn of the century, however, a vituperative Watson was explaining that "in the South, we have to lynch him [the Negro] occasionally, and flog him, now and then, to keep him from blaspheming the Almighty by his conduct, on account of his smell and his color." As far as Watson was concerned, "Lynch law is a good sign: it shows that a sense of justice yet lives among the people."

Watson's hatred did not stop with the blacks whose votes he had once courted but whose disfranchisement he now endorsed. In his newspaper and magazine writings, Watson called the attention of his betrayed and disillusioned Populist brethren to all sorts of Catholic and Jewish conspiracies. Dismissing the pope as a "fat old dago" who consorted with "voluptuous women," he treated his readers to accounts of "What Happens in Convents" and other such revelations.

Watson's bigotry brought out the worst in many of his fellow Georgians. On a summer night in 1915, the Ku Klux Klan was reborn atop Georgia's Stone Mountain. Watson did not attend, but his spirit was clearly there. Watson also played a key role in one of the most tragic episodes in Georgia's history, the lynching of Leo Frank. Frank, a Jew and a northern one at that, was the superintendent at an Atlanta pencil factory. One of his employees, fourteen-year-old Mary Phagan, was found murdered in the basement of the factory on April 27, 1913. Frank admitted to having been at the factory and paying the girl her wages (on a holiday, when the factory was shut down), and he was immediately taken into custody. Though there was a black suspect — later implicated by evidence much stronger than any associated with Frank — public opinion, fanned yet again by the Atlanta press, seized on Frank as the killer, especially after the newspapers ran several examples of Frank's alleged sexual perversion. The police seemed equally committed to the idea of Frank's guilt, and the trial, which lasted thirty days, was conducted in an atmosphere of mob hysteria. Officials feared an acquittal might produce a riot, and court officials received messages such as "Hang the Jew or we will hang you." Not surprisingly, Frank was convicted and sentenced to die.

Every court that reviewed the case expressed doubt as to Frank's guilt, and the verdict was condemned not only in the North and in other parts of the world, but, surprisingly enough, even in southern states such as Tennessee and Texas. Many Georgians quickly grew resentful of this criticism and outside interference in their affairs. The *Atlanta Journal* had called for a new trial, only to back down quickly when its circulation plunged. At this point, Watson plunged into the fray, asserting that "Frank belonged to the Jewish aristocracy, and it was determined by the rich Jews that no aristocrat of their race should die for the death of a working class Gentile." As time passed and Frank's execution was postponed several times, Watson demanded to know, "How much longer is the innocent blood of little Mary Phagan to cry in vain to heaven for vengeance?"

When rumors mounted that outgoing governor John M. Slaton would commute Frank's sentence, Watson headlined his weekly *Jeffersonian* with "RISE! PEOPLE OF GEORGIA." When Slaton did indeed commute the sentence on the day before his term ended, a mob wounded and disabled sixteen of the troopers who had to be called in to protect him, and the ex-governor had no choice but to flee the state. "Our Grand Old Empire State Has Been Raped!" insisted an outraged Watson, who continued to flog the case, warning that "the next Jew who does what Frank did, is going to get exactly the same thing that we give to Negro rapists."

Finally, on August 17, 1915, a mob of twenty-five men entered the state penitentiary in Milledgeville, took Frank out, and drove the back roads all the way to Marietta, where they hanged him from a tree. Clearly well planned, the lynching came off without a hitch. "For audacity and efficiency," wrote historian C. Vann Woodward, "it was unparalleled in southern history." Like countless lynchings of blacks, the grisly affair became both ritual and festival. An estimated fifteen thousand men, women, and children filed past Frank's casket in an Atlanta morgue after officials had been compelled by numerous threats to display it. On the day of the lynching, soon-to-be hillbilly recording star Fiddlin' John Carson stood on the courthouse steps in Marietta all day, playing again and again the "Ballad of Little Mary Phagan":

> Little Mary Phagan
> She went to town one day;
> She went to the pencil factory
> To get her little pay.
>
> Leo Frank met her
> With a brutely heart we know.
> He smiled and said, "Little Mary,
> Now you go home no more. . . ."
>
> Come all of you good people,
> Wherever you may be,
> Supposing little Mary
> Belonged to you or me?

The disturbing image of Georgia embodied in the Leo Frank affair was reinforced by the account of Robert E. Burns, whose 1932 book *I Am a Fugitive from a Georgia Chain Gang!* (and the subsequent film version) only added to the widespread perception of Georgia's benightedness. Given the conditions that prevailed in the state at the time when H. L. Mencken set out in 1931 to identify the "worst American state," many Georgians understandably grew apprehensive. According to Mencken's criteria, of the forty-eight states Georgia ranked forty-fifth in wealth, forty-sixth in education, and forty-third in health. In the "culture" category, Mencken deemed only Arkansas, Alabama, and Mississippi more deficient than Georgia. Meanwhile, in the "public order" category, the tendency of white Georgians to lynch black Georgians put the state in the forty-sixth rank, indicating that only Mississippi and Wyoming were more violent and disorderly. Not surprisingly, Mississippi won Mencken's designation as the "worst" state, but Georgia's boosters could take little comfort in their state's overall ranking of forty-fifth.

At this sad point in its history, Georgia could have served as exhibit A for W. J. Cash's 1941 classic, *The Mind of the South*, a brilliantly executed argument for the existence of a unified and uniquely southern set of values and beliefs that had emerged in the antebellum era, matured and hardened in the crucible of the Civil War and Reconstruction, and persisted without fundamental alteration throughout the first four decades of the twentieth century. Some readers objected to the title of Cash's book because *The Mind of the South* presented an intellectually stagnant, emotionally dysfunctional white South as essentially mindless. As used by Cash, however, "mind" actually referred to an aggregate regional temperament, an indelible, historically and culturally imprinted code of conduct that produced the distinctive and often bizarre behavior that gave the South its peculiar identity. Certainly, Cash's portrait was anything but flattering. His South was one of schizophrenia and excess marked by startling juxtapositions of hedonism and piety and hospitality and violence. More troubling still was Cash's focus on the "savage ideal," a peculiarly southern strain of anti-intellectualism and hostility to criticism or innovation forged during Reconstruction and still the dominant feature of the southern mind more than fifty years later.

Anyone who doubted that Cash's "savage ideal" applied to the "mind" of Georgia's white leadership need only consider the sentiments of the state legislator who spoke out in opposition to a bill allowing local governments to fund public libraries. Acknowledging the need for only three books, Representative Hal Kimberly admonished his constituents: "Read the Bible. It teaches you how to act. Read the hymn-book. It contains the finest poetry ever written. Read the Almanac. It shows you how to figure out what the weather will be. There isn't another book that is necessary for anyone to read, and therefore, I am opposed to all libraries."

THE TALMADGE ERA

Although there were clear deficiencies in the state's social and political systems and its cultural institutions, its most serious deficiencies were economic. Plummeting cotton prices and the general malaise of the Great Depression combined to make Georgia a state whose agriculture showcased the evils of the old plantation system at its pernicious, exploitive worst. Studying Greene and Macon counties, Arthur F. Raper found "depleted soil, shoddy livestock, inadequate farm equipment, crude agricultural practices, crippled institutions, a defeated and impoverished people." Having grown up as one of these people in Bacon County, Georgia, Harry Crews explained their existence in more graphic terms: "Whether on shares or on standing rent, they were still tenant farmers, and survival was a day-to-day crisis as real as the rickets in the bones of their children or the worms that would sometimes rise out of their children's stomachs and nest in their throats so that they had to be pulled out by hand to keep the children from choking."

No writer provided more devastating depictions of southern poor-white life than Georgia's Erskine Caldwell. The son of a socially committed Presbyterian minister, Caldwell grew to share the concerns of his father, who once observed that sharecroppers were "as bad off as a toad in a post hole. It's a disgrace that human beings have to live like that."

Years later, Caldwell described his own observations of the rural poor in Depression-era Georgia: "I could not become accustomed to the sight of children's stomachs bloated from hunger and seeing the ill and aged too weak to walk to the fields to search for something to eat. In the evenings I wrote about what I had seen during the day, but nothing I put down on paper succeeded in conveying the full meaning of poverty and hopelessness and degradation as I had observed it." Perhaps not, but Caldwell's *Tobacco Road*, published in 1932, became a symbol of the evils of the sharecropping system and the ills and suffering endured by a worn-out people trying to live on worn-out soil.

Not everyone in rural and small-town Georgia suffered under the status quo. The pivotal person in the prevailing order in Georgia was described to Ralph McGill as "a certain type, small town rich man." Profiling this figure, McGill explained, "Usually, he lived in the best house, on the best hill in the town, or at the shadiest corner, a block or so off the main street — and always his home sought to sustain the legend of the South as a place of many mansions."

Depending on where he lived, the "small town rich man" owned "the gin, the turpentine works, the cotton warehouses," and "the tobacco warehouses." Wherever he lived, he was invariably "a director in the bank" and the owner of the town's largest store from which he sold "fertilizer, plows, machinery, food, fencing, seeds, patent medicines, poultry and livestock." Beyond that, he or one of his relatives also owned the local automobile dealership.

Financially and politically, he was perfectly positioned: "He controlled credit. He knew the financial predicament of every man in his section of the county. He knew the United States senators, and the congressman from his district was always a 'friend.' He could write to Washington about a job for someone in his community. He could do the same with the governor. . . . He made a contribution at campaign time, always to the right man, and if in doubt, to both candidates. He had a hand in the political patronage in his county. He 'advised,' or selected, the men who ran for the legislature."

The key to the long-standing political preeminence of the small-town rich man was Georgia's county-unit system. Mandated by the legislature in 1917 for use in state primary elections, the county-unit system had traditionally been employed at state Democratic nominating conventions, where delegates voted by counties, each county casting two votes for each representative it elected to the state legislature. Since each county sent at least one representative and no county sent more than three, this system was severely biased against urban counties, and as they grew, the discrimination against them increased proportionately. By way of illustration, in the 1946 gubernatorial primary the county-unit system gave 264 voters in sparsely populated Chattahoochee County the same clout as 28,184 voters in fast-growing Fulton County.

When it came to manipulating the county-unit system and in the process personifying the overwhelming rusticity of Georgia politics, no one ever came close to Eugene Talmadge. Born on the family plantation near Forsyth, Talmadge earned a law degree from the University of Georgia and eventually purchased a farm on Sugar Creek in Telfair County. Claiming to be "a real dirt farmer" and quickly becoming known as "the Wild Man from Sugar Creek," Talmadge upset a powerful incumbent to become commissioner of agriculture in 1926. As commissioner, he proved both flamboyant and reckless. Promising to raise hog prices in Georgia, Talmadge used state funds to purchase hogs for slightly more than the eight-cent-per-pound market price in Georgia with an eye toward shipping them to Chicago, where they could be sold for eleven cents per pound. At his behest, the state dispatched eighty-two carloads of them northward to be offered for sale in Chicago at nine cents per pound. Contrary to Talmadge's claims about the superiority of Georgia swine, however, the poorly fed hogs lost so much weight during the trip that the state suffered a net loss on this venture in excess of ten thousand dollars.

This incident stayed with Talmadge his entire political career, and, ironically, he managed to turn it into more of an asset than a liability. In 1931 the great hog caper resurfaced alongside charges that Talmadge had placed several relatives on his departmental payroll and the disclosure that he had traveled to the Kentucky Derby at state expense. By this time, however, Talmadge had managed so successfully to portray himself as the champion of the little man that his "Shore, I stole, but I stole for you!" explanation was more than sufficient for the majority of his constituents, and the following year when Governor Richard B.

Russell sought and won a seat in the U.S. Senate, Talmadge moved into the governor's mansion.

Talmadge would win the governorship four times, primarily because of his genius for manipulating the emotions of Georgia's rural white electorate and capitalizing on its rurally skewed county-unit system. (Talmadge reportedly bragged that he had never campaigned in a county with a streetcar in it and urged his "country" supporters to come visit him at the governor's mansion and "we'll piss over the rail on those city bastards.") On one level, Talmadge seems an almost comical character. Certainly his rallies appeared to present a caricature of the redneck "wool hat" mentality that prevailed among the white residents of the Georgia countryside in the 1930s and 1940s. "Old Gene" was likely to arrive driving a team of mules or even oxen. Wearing red suspenders, he would mount the platform and work the crowd masterfully. Shunning anything resembling a prepared text, he took his cues from supporters, often "plants" who shouted from the front ranks of the crowd or sometimes from nearby trees: "Tell 'em about them lyin' Atlanta newspapers, Gene." Or, "What about them hogs you stole, Gene?" At the conclusion of Talmadge's performance, a hillbilly band would strike up, and with the corn liquor flowing and the green flies swarming, his supporters would feast on barbecue or fried fish under the broiling Georgia sun.

As a politician and a political leader, Gene Talmadge was always entertaining and often amusing. He was, however, far from harmless. His wooing of the wool hat boys by cutting the price of an automobile license plate in Georgia to three dollars created a tremendous stir, drawing tag purchasers from as far away as Brooklyn and inspiring Fiddlin' John Carson to compose "The Three-Dollar Tag Song" and sing, with the accompaniment of his daughter, "Moonshine Kate":

> I gotta Eugene Dog, I gotta Eugene Cat.
> I'm a Talmadge man from my shoes to my hat.
> Farmer in the corn field hollerin' whoa, gee, haw.
> Kain't put no thirty-dollar tag on a three-dollar car.

Talmadge's goal was to embellish his credentials with the dirt farmers, but the real beneficiaries of his action were the corporations with large fleets of vehicles, while the losers were the local governments in rural areas (which also suffered by Talmadge's efforts to reduce the ad valorem tax rate), because the decrease in tag revenues cut sharply into the state's school fund, forcing hikes in local taxes in order to keep the schools open. Elsewhere, though a self-proclaimed friend of the "working man," Talmadge accepted a twenty-thousand-dollar contribution from textile industry leaders during his 1934 reelection campaign, and on the day after his election, he declared martial law, using the National Guard to break the 1934 textile strike in Georgia and incarcerate the strikers in a hastily constructed camp near Atlanta. In this case, as in many others, Talmadge did not shrink from acting dictatorially or from using troops to back up his actions. When Talmadge's opposition to the New Deal led legislative opponents to block passage of a state appropriations bill in 1936, he declared martial law and summoned National Guardsmen to oust forcibly both the state treasurer and comptroller general. At his order, a welder's torch was brought in to open treasury vaults and remove money.

As the dominant force in Georgia politics for nearly twenty years, Talmadge sometimes seemed invincible. Yet he did operate within limitations, and the setbacks he suffered demonstrated that, contrary to appearances perhaps, Talmadge-era Georgia was undergoing some important changes. For all his popularity within the state, Talmadge got little encouragement when he sought to become a national political figure. A 1936 "grassroots convention" to choose an anti-Roosevelt candidate for the Democratic presidential nomination was supposed to be a political springboard for keynote speaker Talmadge, but despite his first-rate, intensely demagogic performance, support for his candidacy failed to materialize, even in Georgia counties he was considered to have "in his pocket." Talmadge was soundly beaten in his effort to oust Richard B. Russell from the Senate in 1936, and in 1938 when he made a similar run against Georgia's senior senator, Walter F. George, voters largely ignored his campaign, focusing on the battle between George and President Roosevelt's anointed but ill-fated candidate, U.S. district attorney Lawrence Camp. Talmadge's condemnation of the New Deal as a combination of "wet-nursin' frenzied finance and plain damn foolishness" hurt him with voters who viewed both FDR and his program as "a godsend."

Talmadge's indiscretions also cost him politically during his third term as governor. Shortly after his election in 1940, he launched a campaign to purge the state's institutions of higher learning of all "foreign professors trying to destroy the sacred traditions of the South." Talmadge sought to oust the president of the state teachers college at Statesboro and the dean of the College of Education at the University of Georgia. At one point, Talmadge entertained thoughts of ridding the university of all pernicious "furrin" (i.e., non-Georgia) personnel, but when he discovered that this group numbered more than seven hundred, he gave up on the idea. Meanwhile, however, at his behest, various committees searched the state's textbook lists and university libraries for "subversive" publications. In response to these high jinks, the Southern Association of Colleges and Secondary Schools dropped the state's ten white colleges from its accredited list.

In the 1942 gubernatorial election, the first for a four-year term, the *Atlanta Journal* declared Talmadge's reelection candidacy "an insult to Georgia's intelligence" and helped to rally the state's theretofore dormant "better element" against him in his race against Attorney General Ellis G. Arnall. Despite his indulgence in such unfamiliar rhetoric as "academic freedom," Arnall managed to outdistance a disgusted Talmadge, who remarked that for all of his opponent's talk about education, "It ain't never taught a man to plant cotton."

GEORGIA TURNS A CORNER

Indications that times were changing in Georgia grew more pronounced during the World War II years. In 1944 the U.S. Supreme

Court invalidated the white primary, thereby clearing the way for blacks to vote in the 1946 elections. Meanwhile, the CIO (Congress of Industrial Organizations) launched its "Operation Dixie" organizing campaign, challenging Georgia and the South's reputation as a bastion of cheap, docile labor. Within this superheated context, Eugene Talmadge made his final bid for the governor's office. Running against the *Atlanta Constitution*'s anointed candidate, Marietta lawyer and former Bell Bomber plant executive James V. Carmichael, Talmadge and his forces made no secret of their intention to ground their campaign in the defense of white supremacy and the other virtues of the "southern way of life" and to concentrate their efforts on enough rural counties to make the county-unit system work its malapportioned magic one more time. As for the newly enfranchised black voters, Talmadge openly encouraged his supporters to intimidate them, advising that "if the good white people will explain it to the negroes around over the state just right, I don't think they will want to vote." It was surely no mere coincidence that after weeks of listening to Talmadge's race-baiting rhetoric, a mob of Walton County whites lynched two black couples in July 1946, eight days after the primary ballots had been cast. Although he gave lip service to white supremacy and defended the county-unit system, Carmichael was clearly the choice of the state's more affluent urban voters. Predictably, the "lying Atlanta newspapers" cut loose at Talmadge with both barrels. The *Atlanta Journal* branded him a "blatant demagogue," a "panderer to the passions of the ignorant and to the fears of the timid, . . . a blatherskite, a cheap fraud and a menace to the security and the welfare of us all."

When it was all over, Carmichael had garnered a plurality of the popular vote, but true to fashion yet again, Talmadge had made the county-unit system work for him, and on the basis of the unit vote, he won the election. The outcome of the 1946 gubernatorial primary reflected the stalemate that prevailed in a state with one foot in the future and one in the past.

More progressive Georgians had long been concerned about the embarrassment that Gene Talmadge often caused, but little that Talmadge had done in life could compare with the chaos that ensued in the wake of his death in December 1946. Because Talmadge died before taking office, the task of selecting a governor fell by constitutional mandate to the legislature, which was charged with counting the ballots and naming the official winner. If no candidate received a majority, the legislature was to choose between the two receiving the most votes. Anticipating Gene's impending demise, a number of his supporters had organized a general election write-in campaign for his son, Herman, already known throughout the state (whether affectionately or disdainfully) as "Hummon." Hummon's supporters argued that he would be the logical choice, but outgoing governor Ellis G. Arnall insisted that the constitution required him to remain in office "until his successor be chosen and qualified." In Arnall's view, that successor was and should be only the duly elected incoming lieutenant governor, Melvin E. Thompson.

Meanwhile, much to the consternation of the Talmadge camp, the initial vote count showed that 669 hard-core Talmadge haters had written in Carmichael on their general-election ballots. Behind Carmichael came not the younger Talmadge but perennial Republican write-in candidate D. Talmadge Bowers with 637 votes. Herman had apparently received only 619 write-in votes, and because the legislature was to choose from only the top two candidates, it seemed as though the son of Gene Talmadge would be denied the opportunity to succeed his father. As "luck" would have it, however, officials in Talmadge's home county of Telfair made a startling last-second discovery. Some fifty-six write-ins for Herman had been misplaced among the returns for the lieutenant governor's race. Subsequent examination of these newly discovered ballots brought further and even more startling revelations. All of the "misplaced" votes for Talmadge had been cast by dead people, many of whom displayed a remarkably similar handwriting style. As one journalist deadpanned, "They rose from the dead in Telfair County, marched in alphabetical order to the polls, cast their votes for Herman Talmadge, and went back to their last repose."

However extraordinary the circumstances may have seemed to external observers, Herman Talmadge now had 675 votes, and the legislature lost little time in declaring him governor. Arnall refused to vacate the office, and the Talmadge forces kept alive a family tradition by seizing both the governor's office and the mansion itself. Shortly thereafter Arnall passed on his claim to the governorship to Thompson, who set up shop in an office downtown, a sort of ruler-in-exile who had never left the state. Finally, on the order of the state supreme court, Thompson became governor in March 1947, but he served only briefly and ineffectively. Herman Talmadge won a special election in 1948 and sought to assume his father's mantle as the champion of the racial and political status quo in Georgia.

Although it made Georgia the butt of numerous jokes in the national media, the "three governors controversy" marked the beginning of a significantly different if not altogether new era in Georgia politics. Herman Talmadge would go on to be a staunch defender of the "southern way of life" and even claim authorship of a pamphlet entitled *You and Segregation* in which he insisted "GOD ADVOCATES SEGREGATION." He also sponsored a 3 percent sales tax that, not coincidentally, generated the revenues for a last-ditch effort to stave off federal intervention by narrowing the gap between white and black schools. Still, the new tax also greatly enhanced the funding prospects for public education in general, a move that not only educators but increasing numbers of business and political leaders, including the new and at least moderately improved Talmadge in the governor's office, felt was absolutely crucial to the state's economic future. Though he followed his father in portraying himself as the farmer's best friend, Herman Talmadge also became an enthusiastic champion of industrial development as well.

Efforts to bring industry to Georgia had actually begun to intensify during the years after World War I. Although the boll weevil had arrived in Georgia several years earlier, it became a major problem only in the early 1920s. As a reflection of the boll weevil's impact, cotton production fell from 2,122,000 bales in 1918 to 588,000 in 1923. In Greene

County, a crop of 21,500 bales in 1919 dwindled to an astonishing 326 bales in 1922. The boll weevil plague shook Georgia's agricultural order to its very foundations. Nearly two of ten Georgians (almost a half million in all) left the state during the 1920s. The majority of those who fled were black. Meanwhile, by 1930 more than half the state's labor force had undertaken nonagricultural pursuits. With Georgia's farm economy seemingly headed toward collapse, voters had already approved a constitutional amendment allowing local tax exemptions for new factories.

At the same time, manufacturing employment and population growth undergirded an urban boom that seemed wholly incompatible with the economic deterioration of the countryside. A "Forward Atlanta" campaign spotlighted the ascendance of urban Georgia, where three of ten Georgians had taken up residence by 1930. The exodus from the farm continued throughout the 1930s. The New Deal's Agricultural Adjustment Administration (AAA) introduced a program of subsidized acreage reduction, triggering what historian Pete Daniel called "a vast enclosure movement" that swept thousands of Georgians from the land toward an uncertain future either in one of the state's larger towns or cities or, ultimately, in a city north of the Mason-Dixon line. In the AAA's first seven years, Georgia lost 40 percent of its sharecroppers. AAA payments helped to finance the large-scale purchase of tractors that signaled the beginning of the end of the mule's reign as the flesh and blood symbol of southern agriculture.

For many years after they ceased to rely on mules to plant and plow cotton, Georgia farmers hung on to at least one mule to work their gardens until the garden tractor finally completed the process that its larger ancestor had begun. Bemoaning the mule's disappearance from the Georgia landscape, Harry Crews recalled that when he was a boy in South Georgia, "horses were playthings that few people could afford; mules put grits on the table and bought the baby's shoes. From a farmer's point of view, though, one of the best things about a mule is the care he takes about where he puts his feet. He will walk all day long beside cotton that is eight inches high and never step on a hill of it. A horse will step all over it. A horse just doesn't give a damn. If a mule steps on your foot, you can be sure he meant to do it."

The emerging revolution in Georgia agriculture contributed as well to the beginnings of a transformation in the economies of hundreds of small towns across the state. Few of these communities, if any, had an industrial base sufficient, especially in the midst of the Depression, to absorb the swelling surplus of farm labor. In these areas the displaced farm workers promised to contribute little more than names to the relief rolls, and they certainly were incapable of consuming the goods and services that merchants, lawyers, bankers, and insurance agents had to offer. Facing a threat to their own survival, the state's small-town middle class followed in the footsteps of their growth-mad Atlanta brethren in the hopes of rejuvenating their faltering local economies.

Despite New Deal recovery efforts and the expanded crusade for new industry, World War II was the pivotal event in Georgia's economic transformation. Defense expenditures supplied the capital necessary to fuel the more rapid industrialization required to free the state completely from the grips of plantation agriculture and modify a manufacturing sector dominated by cruder, labor- and resource-exploitive "plantation industries." The war brought massive federal spending to Georgia, which was second only to Texas in attracting military training facilities. Fort Benning was the largest infantry training post in the world; Robins Air Force Base employed as many as fifteen thousand civilians at one point. Every major city sported some kind of military installation. Defense-related industry also made a major contribution to the state's economy. At one point, Bell Aircraft in Marietta employed some twenty-eight thousand workers, shipyards flourished in Savannah and Brunswick, and ordnance plants opened in Macon and Milledgeville. The impact of this capital transfusion quickly revealed itself in per capita income, which climbed from less than $350 in 1940 to over $1,000 by 1950.

The mechanization and consolidation of agriculture also accelerated during and after the war. In 1940, six of ten Georgia farms were tenant operated, but by the mid-1950s, only one-third were farmed by non-owners. In the same period, the number of farm tractors rose from fewer than ten thousand to approximately eighty-five thousand. Meanwhile, the mechanical cotton picker had gone into mass production in 1948. Twenty years later, it was harvesting nearly 90 percent of Georgia's up-land cotton crop. As mechanization made it easier and more efficient to farm more land and harder for small farmers without the necessary implements to compete, average farm size grew by nearly 80 percent between 1945 and 1959, while over the same period the total number of farms fell by more than 50 percent. Cotton had grown on more than five million acres in Georgia on the eve of World War I, and on the eve of World War II, it had still produced nearly 40 percent of all farm income. This figure was down to 10 percent by the end of the 1950s, however, as continuing struggles with the boll weevil and low prices spurred farmers to turn cropland into pastures for livestock and move into poultry production as well.

At the end of World War II, Georgia stood on the brink of an era of economic, political, and social modernization. Low-wage industries like textiles, apparel, and lumber and wood products continued to dominate, but the income growth of the war years began to attract the attention of some more market-oriented industries as well. Per capita income approached 70 percent of the national average by 1950 with much of the state's growth centering in Atlanta, where income already surpassed the national figure. The Georgia capital became a magnet for companies seeking access to Georgia's and the Southeast's burgeoning consumer markets. The automobile industry found the city a prime lo-cation, and the list of its other new firms began to show a solid Fortune 500 presence.

If preserving white supremacy was the foremost responsibility of Georgia's governor during the 1950s and early 1960s, recruiting new industry was running an increasingly closer second. Hence Geor-gia's governors during the period were both super-segregationists and super-salesmen. As Governor S. Ernest Vandiver explained, "If you send an industrial representative to these places, he talks to his counterpart in the business, but a governor — any governor — gets to the president and chairman of the board where the final decisions are made."

As the likelihood of civil rights conflict grew, the efforts of Georgia's governors to woo new industry took on definite sectional overtones. In 1952 when the governor of Rhode Island complained of "raiding" by southern governors, Governor Herman Talmadge escalated the rhetorical combat, vowing, "If he wants war, we'll give him war." Back home in Georgia, the newspapers reported on the governor's industry-seeking forays to the North much as if he were a latter-day J. E. B. Stuart conducting a daring raid behind enemy lines.

The desire of Georgia's political leaders to promote economic change while preserving the racial status quo was not so contradictory as it seemed. Like the rest of the southern states, Georgia found its primary appeal to industrial investors was its presumably inexhaustible supply of "100 percent Anglo Saxon" workers so desperate for work of any sort that they would be grateful for even the meagerest of wages. The phrase "100 percent Anglo Saxon" not only implied white — most plants coming to Georgia during this period hired blacks only for the most menial and distasteful jobs — but native-born workers, presumably more resistant than their northern immigrant counterparts to the entreaties of union organizers. Indeed, Georgia was (and, to a surprising extent, remains) a bastion of antiunionism. Not only did Gene Talmadge use the state militia to break strikes, but the state legislature passed a rigid right-to-work law. At the local level, towns such as Sandersville, Baxley, and others required unions to pay a two-thousand-dollar license fee plus five hundred dollars for each local resident they recruited. When challenging the constitutionality of such a statute in Cuthbert, CIO representative Lucy Randolph Mason reportedly asked the city court judge (who was also the mayor) whether he believed in the Bill of Rights. When he asked her, "What is the Bill of Rights?" Mason directed his attention to the U.S. Constitution and its guarantee of the freedom of peaceable assembly. "We don't need any of that in Cuthbert," the mayor/judge responded. "The only laws we know are local laws."

Surely, the gentleman would have recognized the state's antiunion right-to-work law, passed in 1947, but much of the real resistance to unions had little to do with the law in any event. Across most of the state, it was always open season on union workers as law-enforcement officials either looked the other way or joined in when would-be organizers were harassed, beaten, or run out of town. Blatant hatred of unions was an altogether respectable bias, even among the state's more reputable businessmen and development promoters. In 1965 the state Chamber of Commerce published a flier entitled "Take a Tip from the Beaver, Mr. Businessman," urging employers to band together to resist unionization efforts in their area. When industrialists looked at a potential site, the pamphlet warned, their first question was often "How many unions are nearby?" With only 14 percent (less than half the national average) of the state's nonagricultural workers carrying union cards in 1964, in Georgia, the answer was clearly "Not many."

Dogged resistance to unionization went hand-in-hand with the progressively intensifying and expanding effort to create new industrial jobs at any and all costs. For many years, Georgia communities had been courting industries through the use of all sorts of favors and financial incentives. A 1937 survey revealed that Douglasville had not only provided a free building for a garment factory, but had paid the employees while they learned their jobs and had given the company a five-year exemption from local taxes as well. Meanwhile, Washington, Georgia, had landed a shirt factory by collecting twenty thousand dollars through public subscription and promising to match this with funds amassed by wage deductions from the plant's workers, who had signed promissory notes in order to get jobs that would pay them, on average, about five dollars a week.

Although development experts frowned on such reckless and unregulated activities, by the 1960s the state of Georgia had a full arsenal of development incentives including tax-free bond financing for new industrial buildings and a host of other provisions deemed likely to lure more manufacturing jobs to a Georgia location. Throughout the state, communities large and small had organized various development groups aimed at facilitating their transformation from farm market and processing centers into full-fledged industrial behemoths. More Georgians already worked in manufacturing than in agriculture in 1950, and manufacturing employment rose by 27 percent over the next decade. Yet for most of Georgia's towns and some of its cities, the primary selling point remained a large pool of cheap, unskilled labor, a reality reflected in the state's industrial base. In 1958, with a paycheck of $60.45, the average Georgia factory worker was earning $22 less each week than his northern counterpart. As of the mid-1960s, more than 75 percent of the workforce in 76 of the state's 159 counties was still employed in the textile, apparel, and lumber and wood-products industries. In 1950 low-wage industries had accounted for 83 percent of the state's manufacturing jobs. By 1970 this figure was down to 67 percent before eventually stabilizing at around 60 percent over the next twenty years.

THE PRICE OF PROGRESS

Although economic and political leaders had long insisted that industrial development would be the state's salvation, the damage that it inflicted on the environment of a state whose pristine beauty had captivated scores of visitors seemed a high price to pay, even in the name of "progress." In their efforts to entice industry to Georgia, state and local officials had offered cheap labor and also free and essentially untrammeled access to the state's natural resources. Not surprisingly, this approach led to some serious examples of exploitation and abuse. When the Union Camp Corporation came to Depression-weary Savannah in 1935, local leaders not only promised nominal rents and protection from competition but pledged as well "to secure the necessary action and, if possible, legislation on the part of the governmental bodies concerned, to protect and save you [Union Bag] harmless from any claims, demands or suits for the pollution of air or water caused by the operation of the plant." Furthermore, Savannah's officials agreed that "in case litigation arises or suits are brought against you on account of odors and/or flowage from the proposed plant that the Industrial Committee of Savannah will pay all expenses of defending such suits up to a total amount of $5,000."

Such hospitality to pulp and paper mills explained why several generations of Florida-bound northern tourists instinctively thought of Georgia whenever they smelled rotten eggs. Concentrated in the southern and coastal counties, the pulp and paper industry alone released millions of pounds of toxic pollutants into the air and water each year. Given that as late as 1960 some 70 percent of all the state's municipal sewage also flowed untreated directly into local streams, it is hardly surprising that inspectors found the oxygen supply so depleted in the waters of the lower Savannah that only the "hardiest" fish could survive. Federal agencies and a smattering of environmental activists occasionally managed to push Georgia's legislature to take corrective action, but to chamber of commerce officials, the stench of the paper mills and other forms of industrial contamination was simply "the smell of jobs," and through threats of plant closings and skillful legal maneuverings, some of the state's worst polluters managed to avoid the most stringent measures needed to clean up their acts entirely. In 1967, after a fairly strong air-pollution-control measure died in committee, a replacement bill, actually proposed by a Union Camp representative, sailed through the legislature with only a few changes. The new law authorized only such pollution control as was "consistent with providing for maximum employment and the full industrial development of the state" and prevented the Georgia Air Quality Branch from inconveniencing Union Camp and other paper companies by forbidding the burning of forest land.

While the rest of the state remained largely the captive of a low-wage, often "dirty," industrial economy, the Atlanta area surged ahead. As novelist Anne Rivers Siddons wrote, in the "headlong, heart-spinning, gold-bitten, high-bouncing decade" of the 1960s, "there was no place on earth like Atlanta." By 1970 the five-county metropolitan area accounted for 33 percent of the state's people, 38 percent of its jobs, and 42 percent of its personal income. This pattern of concentrated, uneven growth played a key role in bringing sweeping social and political changes to Georgia. Urban-rural tensions had begun to simmer well before Gene Talmadge had emerged as the dominant figure on Georgia's political scene. A noted historian had concluded in 1934 that not only did rural Georgia actually have "little tangible connection" with Atlanta but that "the city is quite evidently not proud of Georgia." As the civil rights era unfolded, not even the most casual observer could fail to see that the interests, aims, and ambitions of Atlanta's most influential political and economic leaders were dramatically different in many ways from those that prevailed in the state at large.

In the wake of the 1954 *Brown v. Board of Education* school desegregation decision, the majority of white Georgians and their representatives in the legislature vowed to close the public schools rather than accept integration. Elected governor in 1954 to succeed Herman Talmadge (although he seemed more reminiscent of Gene), S. Marvin Griffin assailed the "meddling demagogues, race-baiters, and Communists" who were "determined to destroy every vestige of state's rights" and swore to defend "Georgia's two greatest traditions — segregation and the county-unit system." In 1958 Griffin's successor, Ernest Vandiver, seemed equally defiant when he promised that "no not one!" black would be educated with whites during his term as governor. The following year, when a federal court ordered desegregation of the Atlanta public schools, the likelihood of school closings loomed large. Rather than opt for this course immediately, however, the legislature created a special committee to study the matter and report back to them in 1961. Although the majority of white Georgians seemed ready to close the schools, many leaders of Atlanta's business community believed such action would be disastrous for their city's economic future. It was particularly significant, therefore, that the special legislative committee was chaired by influential Atlanta banker John A. Sibley. The committee held hearings in each of the state's ten congressional districts, listening to some eighteen hundred witnesses, all but two hundred of whom were white. Despite claims that 55 percent of those interviewed had favored school closings, Sibley and a majority of the committee recommended local option on the matter of choosing between closing the schools or operating them on an integrated basis.

Meanwhile, even as the Sibley Commission prepared its report, the state faced its first real confrontation on integration, not in Atlanta but in Athens, when a federal court ordered the immediate admission of black applicants Charlayne Hunter and Hamilton Holmes to the University of Georgia. There was talk of closing the university, but despite a nasty campus riot, the crisis gradually eased. The sacred principle of Jim Crow had been breached, and yet the university still functioned, and the sun still rose over one end of Sanford Stadium and set over the other.

Both the Sibley Report and the decision to keep the University of Georgia open reflected the long reach and deep pockets of the Atlanta business and financial community. Indeed, the integration of Atlanta's public schools in the fall of 1961 proved anticlimactic and uneventful. Plans for just such an outcome had been painstakingly laid by longtime mayor William B. Hartsfield, who had already been telling all who would listen that his beloved, dynamic Atlanta was simply "too busy to hate." The city was deluged with reporters as the schools opened, but there was, in fact, little to report, and the irrepressible Hartsfield arranged for these journalists to take a bus tour in order to see, among other things, the city's "fine Negro homes." Afterward, he hosted a cocktail party for the visiting press, including Charlayne Hunter, who had recently broken the color barrier at the University of Georgia.

The well-publicized events in Atlanta and Athens notwithstanding, as the 1960s began, whites and blacks in rural Georgia continued to interact with each other in much the same fashion as they had been for nearly a century. Georgia novelist and social critic Lillian Smith believed that most southern white children were taught "to love God, to love one's white skin, and to believe in the sanctity of both." Smith's 1944 novel, *Strange Fruit*, was a searing story of miscegenation and murder that concluded with the lynching of an innocent young black man. Reflecting on the lynching, an elderly white woman is obsessed with the smell of the young man's burning flesh, while a poor white who lost both his legs in a sawmill accident finds his sexual potency restored by this grisly reassertion of white supremacy. No segment of the book has greater force, however, than Smith's treatment of the relationship between Tracy Deen, a young white boy, and Henry McIntosh, the son of Tracy's family's housekeeper, who will eventually be lynched for Tracy's murder.

Black or white, every child who grew up in the Jim Crow South recalls vividly the first time he or she discovered that, despite their physical proximity, playmates of different colors lived by different rules. Smith captured the trauma of this discovery in an incident that occurs when Henry is eight and Tracy seven and the two are playing on the sidewalk. When Henry refuses to yield to a young white girl on a tricycle, a collision results. Both Henry and Tracy laugh, but Mamie, Henry's mother, does not:

Mamie whipped her boy. She whipped him, saying, "I got to learn it to you, you heah! I got to. You can't look at a white gal like dat, you can't tech one, you can't speak to one cep to say yes mam and thanky mam. Say it atter me. Say it!" And Henry, squalling and catching his breath in strangling gasps, said it after her, word for word, three times, as she urged him on, tapping his legs with the tip of the switch as he said it. Then black legs whitened by the lash of his lesson, snuffling and dazed, he ran into the cabin and like a shamed dog crawled under the bed.

Mamie's big brown hands took the switch and slowly broke it to pieces. . . . She stood there staring across the roof of the big yellow house in front of her. Stared so long that the small white boy watching her thought she must not be able to find what she looked for. . . . "Mamie," Tracy had said the word with no idea behind it, "Mamie."

She looked up, brown face wet with her crying, and twisted. "Go!" she said, "Go to your own folks." she said. And he turned and ran quickly, cut to the bone by the new strange words.

Like Tracy, I grew up in a segregated, race-dominated South, living in the midst of blacks but often wholly apart from them. The entirety of my twelve years of education in Hart County, Georgia, was spent in all-white public schools. I recall vividly the cold rainy mornings during my early school years when I boarded the bus for Nancy Hart Elementary School (a brand new building as of my third-grade year), while the black children who lived around me trooped up the road on foot to get their education at Colored Zion School, a two-room ramshackle building in what had once been a cotton field. The threat of integration brought consolidation and the construction of the new Hart County Training School for blacks, but my alma mater, Hart County High School, was not integrated until the fall of 1965, the year I went on to the University of Georgia.

As I reflect on all the racial inequities that I observed as a youth, I cannot help feeling ashamed that I raised no objections and relatively few questions about the way things were. While neither of my parents was a racial egalitarian by any stretch of the imagination, both seemed, from my perspective, at least, to treat black people as decently as the prevailing codes of caste etiquette would allow. My father regularly lent money to blacks who came seeking it. Though he charged no interest, he expected them to pay him back eventually and to be available to help

him or my mother when they called them. On such occasions, I observed that my parents often "paid" their black helpers with old clothes
or shoes rather than cash. I noticed that the response to this form of
payment was often less than enthusiastic, but when I asked my parents
about it, they assured me that their black neighbors much preferred
having a good warm (if old) coat to receiving a few dollars (which they
would probably only "throw away" in any event). Somehow, even then,
I doubted this priority, but I also knew that a black couple down the
road had named one of their sons for my father and one of their daughters for my mother. I also observed that every summer, when the now-
adult offspring of many local black families returned from their homes
"up North," they always stopped by to see my folks, and there seemed to
be genuine pleasure taken in these visits by all those involved. Even on
these occasions there were inconsistencies and contradictions. While
our black visitors always called my father "Mr. Joel" and my mother
"Miss Modena," I had never heard my parents or any other whites use
these titles when addressing or referring to blacks.

It was impossible to overlook the general impoverishment of our
black neighbors, but I often heard whites attribute this to "sorriness" or
irresponsibility. Beyond that, I was hardly wallowing in affluence myself, living in a small frame house with no underpinning or even indoor
plumbing. (The latter came when I was twelve. I rejoiced at no longer
having to bathe in a washtub on the back porch or brave the black widows and snakes in our old outhouse, but more than that, in my own ju-
venile way, I felt a vague satisfaction in having finally joined the middle
class.)

Only when I was a few years older did I begin to understand the
economic implications of race. My father had given a friend of his the
hay off our pasture in order to get the pasture mowed. When the friend
asked me if I would like to work a half day, helping him and his hired
hand, a middle-aged black man named Boston Gaines, to get the hay
up, I eagerly agreed, since I had planned a big trip to a nearby county
fair that evening. We began around noon and worked until six p.m. or

even after. Though a robust country lad, I was unaccustomed to such labor and was totally exhausted by "quittin' time" when my father's friend approached me and, nodding toward his black helper, asked, "Be all right if I pay you same as Boston?" "Yessir," I blurted out, thinking this only fair, after all. With that, he handed me the princely sum of $2.50, exactly half of what he paid his black employee for a twelve-hour day. Somehow, I managed to thank him, though I was totally stunned. I had gotten myself through the punishing afternoon only by thinking of all the money I would have to spend at the fair. I did go to the fair, where I quickly spent my hard-earned $2.50. (I forget on just what, but I do remember thinking, "Well, there goes a half day's pay.") Later, when I complained to my father about his friend's lack of generosity, he only shook his head and pointed out that I had agreed to accept the same pay as Boston. Clearly, this incident stuck with me, although it was some time before I actually grasped the lesson it should have taught me on the spot.

Change did not come easily or rapidly to the society in which I grew up, yet in 1946 (the year before I was born), a truly remarkable Georgian, Katharine Du Pre Lumpkin, saw in the contemporary scene "the old life continuing, yet a rising tide against it." The self-described "daughter of an eloquent father, reared in a home where the Confederacy is revered as a cause, holy and imperishable," Lumpkin graduated from Brenau College in Gainesville and went on to earn a Ph.D. in economics from the University of Wisconsin. Her family's move to the sand hills of South Carolina afforded her the chance to observe the poverty and struggle of poor whites. Later, her collegiate involvement with the interracial activities of the YWCA (Young Women's Christian Association) led her to realize that race "was nonexistent, only a fiction, a myth, which white minds had created for reasons of their own" and that "wage-earning whites and Negroes were, functionally speaking, not so unlike after all." As she surveyed the South of 1946, Lumpkin noted that the cumulative impact of depression, war, agricultural mechanization, and industrial development was weakening the region's resistance to racial change.

As she looked back from the perspective of 1980, however, Lumpkin realized that black southerners had played the key role in the South's transformation: "The protest movement furnished incontrovertible evidence to any and all who had failed to comprehend, that black people were asserting that the time was now for an end to their burden of discrimination and segregation."

In Georgia, the sit-in movement began in Atlanta in 1960 and spread across the state, affecting almost all of the state's cities of any size. The most widely publicized white-black confrontation in the state during the civil rights era came in and around Albany in Southwest Georgia. Student Nonviolent Coordinating Committee (SNCC) volunteers arrived in the fall of 1961 to begin a voter registration drive, and Albany was soon the scene of the largest black protest effort since the Montgomery bus boycott. In retrospect, the "Albany Movement" represented a turning point in the civil rights crusade as large numbers of working-class blacks joined student organizers and activists in what would become the prototype for later protests in Birmingham and other cities. The Albany campaign led to mass arrests, and as local jails bulged, the overflow of the prisons spilled out to lockups in outlying counties. Inside the jails, demonstrators were often subjected to all kinds of abuse.

SNCC workers who fanned out from Albany faced an even more hostile reception in Terrell County, where beatings, bombings, and drive-by shootings were commonplace. Such terrorism, reminiscent of the Reconstruction era, no longer sufficed to maintain the status quo. A pivotal figure in the Albany Movement, Charles Sherrod endured numerous beatings and threats, but he reported back to SNCC headquarters in Atlanta that "the structure is being shaken to the very foundations. . . . It is no longer a matter-of-fact procedure for a Negro to respond in 'yes, sirs' and 'no, sirs.' The people are thinking. They are becoming. In a deep Southwest Georgia area, where it is generally conceded that the Negro has no rights that a white man is bound to respect, at last, they sing, 'We Shall Overcome.' There is hope!"

Across the state, the sit-in movement attracted large numbers of blacks and a few whites. In Augusta, a white power structure, fearful of the prospect of demonstrations during the Masters golf tournament, acquiesced to peaceful desegregation of lunch counters and theaters in the spring of 1962. In Augusta, as in Atlanta, the desire for economic growth had played a key role in the initial desegregation of public facilities.

A GEORGIAN AND HIS DREAM

When asked why he and his cohorts had capitulated so readily to local blacks' integration demands, a white political leader in Augusta explained, "We were afraid they'd bring in Martin Luther King." Such comments were echoed again and again across Georgia and throughout the South. Though he went on to study at Crozer Theological Seminary and Boston University, Martin Luther King Jr. was, more than anything else perhaps, a product of his Georgia heritage. His father had made his way to Atlanta and worked his way through Morehouse College to become pastor of Ebenezer Baptist Church. The young King grew up in relatively comfortable middle-class circumstances, secure in his parents' love and insulated to some extent from the injuries that the Jim Crow system could so easily inflict. King's father set a stern but courageous example, correcting whites who called him "boy," refusing to allow his children to use segregated public transportation or attend segregated theaters, and encouraging other blacks to register to vote.

His father's dignity as well as the strength of his family's ties to the black religious community (his maternal grandfather was a minister as well) and the strength of the King family itself left young Martin secure in his own racial identity. That security was not allowed to go entirely untested in Jim Crow Georgia, however. As a high school student, King participated in an oratorical contest in Dublin. Returning that evening to Atlanta on the bus, King and his chaperone were ordered to surrender their seats to white passengers, and when they failed to move quickly enough, the driver began cursing, calling them "black sons of bitches." Forced to stand for the remainder of the ninety-mile ride back to Atlanta, King later wrote, "That night will never leave my memory."

Ironically, it was segregation on public buses that would vault King, then a young minister in Montgomery, into the national spotlight. King understood that segregation warped southerners of both races, and he showed a remarkable genius for making his efforts to bring it to an end seem beneficial to whites as well. Drawing on the teachings of Mohandas Gandhi, King cited the moral responsibility of disobeying unjust laws. He praised student demonstrators, noting that "when these disinherited children of God sat down at lunch counters, they were in reality standing up for what is best in the American dream and for the sacred values in our Judeo-Christian heritage."

As headquarters for King's Southern Christian Leadership Conference, Atlanta served as King's base of operations, and even as he became a national and global figure, he remained a Georgian. He invoked the "red clay hills of Georgia" in his famous "I have a dream" speech during the march on Washington. King is probably best remembered for his eloquence on this occasion, but his most impressive composition was his "Letter from a Birmingham Jail," written in response to a statement from a group of moderate white ministers in Birmingham who had urged King and his followers to be more patient with the pace of racial change in their city. King's carefully crafted reply was passionate and, to a great many previously uncommitted readers, highly persuasive as well:

Perhaps it is easy for those who have never felt the stinging darts of segregation to say, "Wait." But when you have seen vicious mobs lynch your mothers and fathers at will and drown your sisters and brothers at whim; when you have seen hate-filled policemen curse, kick, brutalize and even kill your black brothers and sisters with impunity; when you see the vast majority of your twenty million Negro brothers smothering in an airtight cage of poverty in the midst of an affluent society; when you suddenly find your tongue twisted and your speech stammering as you seek to explain to your six-year-old daughter why she can't go to the public amusement park . . . and see tears welling up in her little eyes . . . ; when you take a cross-country drive and find it necessary to sleep night after night in the uncomfortable corners of your automobile because no motel will accept you; . . . when your first name becomes "nigger," and your middle name becomes "boy" . . . and your last name becomes "John," and when your wife and mother are never given the respected title "Mrs."; . . . when you are forever fighting a degenerating sense of "nobodiness"; then you will understand why we find it difficult to wait.

Although he had his share of detractors, King is surely Georgia's most widely admired public figure. Several years after his assassination, another Georgian, novelist Alice Walker, praised him for making it possible for her and millions of other southern blacks to feel at home in the land of their birth: "He was the One, The Hero, The one fearless Person for whom we had waited. . . . He gave us back our heritage. He gave us back our homeland; the bones and dust of our ancestors, who may now sleep within our caring and our hearing. . . . He . . . restored our memories to those of us who were forced to run away, as realities we might each day enjoy and leave for our children. He gave us continuity of place, without which community is ephemeral. He gave us home."

REVOLUTION AND REACTION

The civil rights revolution allowed Georgia blacks to reclaim not only their homeland but their political rights as well. As of 1964 scarcely more than one-fourth of Georgia's voting-age blacks had been registered to vote. Blacks represented 34 percent of the voting-age population, but in the entire state there were only three black elected officials, all of them elected during the preceding three years. The Voting Rights Act of 1965 brought sweeping changes to the state's political landscape. In 1970 the state had roughly thirty black elected officials. By 1990 there were nearly five hundred, and black registration had increased by 80 percent since 1964. These changes had not come without considerable resistance and defensive maneuvering by white politicians who engineered shifts to at-large elections, majority-vote requirements, and other ruses likely to dilute the black vote. Various litigation efforts and pressures from the U.S. Justice Department gradually brought relief in these areas. The federally coerced creation of black-majority voting districts contributed significantly to an increase in black officeholding, although critics charged, with some justification, that this tactic simply created predominantly white districts elsewhere, districts likely to elect representatives hostile to black progress. Statewide, black voters played a key role in ousting Herman Talmadge from the U.S. Senate in 1980, but black candidates generally fared poorly with white voters. In 1981 former ambassador to the United Nations Andrew Young got less than 9 percent of the white vote in winning the mayoral election in Atlanta. In the 1990 gubernatorial primary runoff, Young received less than 26 percent of the white vote.

Social, political, and emotional empowerment often went hand in hand, but they came more rapidly for some black Georgians than for others. When Macon native Melissa Fay Greene arrived as a VISTA (Volunteers in Service to America) Legal Services worker in McIntosh County in 1975, she found that, despite its Reconstruction-era history as a black enclave presided over by Tunis G. Campbell, the civil rights movement seemed to have bypassed the area entirely. She also found a coastal backwater where many of the county's four thousand blacks still spoke Gullah, a synthesis of English, Scottish, and African dialects. Ten years after the passage of the Voting Rights Act of 1965, though blacks accounted for half the county's population, they had not elected a single black public official. In *Praying for Sheetrock*, Greene described the changes that came to McIntosh County as the black community finally awakened to its political potential. The story was one of inspiration and disappointment, courage and corruption (especially in the pivotal case of black activist Thurnell Alston), but in her final assessment,

Greene concluded, "Of course, it is not enough, but it is a beginning. The descendants of the Scottish settlers start to view the descendants of the African slaves not as aliens in their midst, and not as servants, but as neighbors, colleagues, partners, fellow Americans and increasingly, as leaders, as a rich human community without whom McIntosh County — financially, among the poorest counties in Georgia — would be halved, bereft, and truly poorer than any chart could document."

Most Georgia whites did not take kindly to the changes wrought by the civil rights movement, as their astonishing political about-face made clear. Buoyed by a "white backlash" against Democratic support for civil rights legislation and his own opposition to the Civil Rights Act of 1964, Republican Barry Goldwater captured 54 percent of the votes in the 1964 presidential election in a state where nearly two-thirds of the votes had gone to Democrat John F. Kennedy just four years earlier. Running as a third-party candidate, in 1968 Alabama's fiery segregationist George C. Wallace won a 43 percent plurality in Georgia, with only 27 percent of the ballots going to the Democratic candidate, Hubert H. Humphrey. Republican Richard Nixon had managed only 30 percent of the vote himself, but coming on the heels of Goldwater's showing four years earlier, Wallace's performance in Georgia helped to persuade Nixon that, in the future, a GOP "southern strategy" of appealing to racially disenchanted white voters would definitely pay off. Four years later, against the admittedly hapless George McGovern, Nixon got three of every four votes cast in Georgia.

GEORGIA TURNS ANOTHER CORNER

If the civil rights movement and the white reaction thereto seemed to revolutionize Georgia politics, it was arguably no more significant than the Supreme Court's 1962 *Baker v. Carr* decision, which set a precedent for federal court intervention in state legislative apportionment disputes and thus paved the way for the courts to invalidate the county-unit system. The outcome of the University of Georgia's integration crisis and the Sibley Commission report had already signaled the political ascendance of Georgia's, and especially Atlanta's, urban business elite, and the court's ruling suggested that their perch atop the state's political pyramid might soon be even more secure.

The 1962 gubernatorial primary, the first election to be affected by the decision, proved to be a fitting contest for such a role, for it pitted a proponent of the new, urban, growth-oriented ideology against a bona fide representative of Georgia's Talmadge-haunted old order. Handsome, articulate Augusta lawyer Carl E. Sanders promised growth and harmony and explained, "I am a segregationist but not a damn fool." Sanders's opponent was none other than former governor Marvin Griffin, who again made the defense of segregation at all costs the cornerstone of his campaign. The apparent philosophy of Griffin's somewhat ethically challenged first administration had been aptly summarized by one journalist as "if-you-ain't-for-stealing-you-ain't-for-segregation," and as he surveyed the residue of Griffin's fiscal recklessness, his successor, Ernest Vandiver, had complained, "The state of Georgia was buying rowboats that would not float. Some were wisely sent to parks without lakes."

The flamboyant Griffin promised rural whites he would "put Martin Luther King so far back in the jail that you have to pump air to him," but this election was to be decided by popular, not unit, votes, and Sanders's sweep of the metropolitan areas put him in the governor's office. Analysts of all sorts hailed Sanders's triumph as a victory for the urban moderates over the rural traditionalists, but for the defeated Griffin, so legend has it, the key to understanding his demise lay not in demographic analysis but in the simple, sobering reality that "some of the people that ate my barbecue didn't vote for me."

In his inaugural address, Sanders proclaimed, "This is a new Georgia. . . . A Georgia on the threshold of new greatness." Sanders's proclamation may not have been wrong, but it was certainly premature. Sanders recognized the need to upgrade education at all levels in Georgia, and his efforts produced impressive and sweeping improvements in teacher salaries, facilities, and scholarship programs. As governor, Sanders also stressed economic growth, but the 1966 election suggested that the old era was not quite over in Georgia. In the Democratic primary, former Atlanta restaurateur Lester G. Maddox outdistanced former governor Ellis Arnall. Maddox had won the hearts of many of Georgia's nonmetropolitan whites by waving an ax handle in the faces of pickets at his segregated Pickrick restaurant in Atlanta, and for the most part, he was not perceived, for better or worse, as much of an Atlantan. Signs proclaiming "Maddox Country" adorned trees and telephone poles from Hahira to Hiawassee and the entirety of rural and small-town Georgia that lay in between. A high school dropout, the feisty Maddox was known as "ol' Ax Handle" to many admiring whites who turned out to vote for him in huge numbers.

Maddox's candidacy was by no means the only novelty in the 1966 election. Democratic dominance had been a way of life in Georgia since the late nineteenth century. Outside Atlanta and a few old Unionist strongholds in the mountains, Republicans were so rare that they constituted little more than a source of amusement or object of idle curiosity for the great mass of "yellow dog" Democrats who made up the overwhelming majority of the Georgia electorate. In reaction to the civil rights initiatives of the Kennedy and Johnson administrations, however, Georgia whites joined their counterparts elsewhere across the Deep South in deserting the party of their fathers in droves during the presidential election of 1964.

Hence it was hardly surprising that, for the first time since Reconstruction, Georgia Republicans put a serious contender on the 1966 gubernatorial ballot in the person of Congressman Howard "Bo" Callaway, scion of a wealthy textile dynasty near LaGrange. Callaway was clearly the uptown candidate, favored by business interests and suburban whites, but though more discreet than his opponent, he was hardly a crusading integrationist. Illustrative of the similarities and differences between Maddox and Callaway was a story widely circulated during the campaign. It seems that two old South Georgia white men were debating the relative merits of the two candidates. One asserted, "Well, I'm voting for Lester, cause he's ag'in the blacks." "But Bo's ag'in the blacks, too!" the other responded. "Yeah," countered the first, "but Bo thinks ever' body who don't make $20,000 a year is black."

When the votes were counted, the results were predictable. Callaway carried middle- and upper-income white areas, while Maddox swept the blue-collar and rural white votes. As a result of an organized write-in campaign for Arnall, neither candidate received the majority required for election, and twenty years after the infamous "three governors controversy," the legislature once again found itself choosing the governor. Since 230 of the 259 members of the general assembly were Democrats, the choice was really never in doubt. Perhaps the most unlikely candidate ever to win the Georgia governorship, Maddox assessed his accomplishment: "It really wasn't too difficult to be elected. All that was necessary was to defeat the Democrats, the Republicans — on the state and national level — 159 courthouses, more than 400 city halls, the railroads, the utility companies, major banks and major industry, and all the daily newspapers and TV stations in Georgia."

Most political observers predicted the worst. Rev. Martin Luther King Jr. saw Maddox's triumph as "indicative of a deep corroding cancer in the Georgia body politic. Georgia is a sick state produced by the disease of a sick nation. I must confess that Mr. Maddox's victory causes me to be ashamed to be a Georgian."

Maddox was none too anxious to claim common citizenship with King, either. He referred consistently to King's "communistic" activities, and at King's death, having called in state troopers to protect the capitol, he gave them orders, in the event of violence, to "shoot them down and stack them up." Such statements were all too typical. Thankfully, Maddox was not as bad a governor as most had expected. He appointed more blacks to state posts than had his predecessors, and he also proved generous in his support for education. Yet although he remained popular with less-affluent white Georgians, Maddox failed to create anything resembling an effective working relationship with the general assembly. He also insisted on continuing to preach the gospel of segregationism and condemned his opponents and critics as communists and cowards. Still, Maddox hardly left office in disgrace, or certainly in any more disgrace than he had entered it. He was, after all, resoundingly elected to the office of lieutenant governor in 1970 and managed in that capacity to make considerable trouble for his successor.

As he laid plans to succeed Maddox, former state senator Jimmy Carter of Plains took note of the strength of the governor's support among rural whites. Accordingly, his gubernatorial campaign bore both racial and class overtones as he openly courted the supporters of Maddox and former presidential hopeful George Wallace and attacked his principal opponent, former governor Carl E. Sanders, as "Cufflinks Carl," an elitist country-club liberal, out of touch with the concerns of the so-called common man.

Upon taking office, however, Carter changed his tune and perhaps even ushered in the "new era" that his defeated opponent had hailed prematurely some eight years earlier. Carter set the tone for his governorship as soon as he was sworn in, telling Georgians, "quite frankly, the time for racial discrimination is over. . . . No poor, rural, weak, or black person should ever have to bear the additional burden of being deprived of the opportunity of an education, a job, or simple justice." Both symbolically and substantively, Carter followed through on his inaugural address, making an impressive number of black appointments and hanging a portrait of Rev. Martin Luther King Jr. in the capitol. Carter also went on to sponsor an extensive agenda of governmental reorganization and judicial and penal reform.

A GEORGIAN IN THE WHITE HOUSE

As of the mid-1970s, Georgians could point with pride to many positive changes that had come to their state in recent years. Yet for all this improvement, a certain inferiority complex lingered. Georgia-born humorist Roy Blount Jr. explained: "Georgia is a place you get sent to or you come from or you march through or you drive through. Convicts settled it. It's got some fine red dirt, hills, vegetables and folks, but I don't believe anybody has ever dreamed of growing up and moving to Georgia." Although not altogether accurate historically, Blount's penetrating observation helped to explain why Georgians were stunned and delighted (initially at least) with the election of one of their own to the presidency in 1976. An engineer-turned-agribusinessman-turned-politician, Jimmy Carter stepped into the void of confidence induced by the back-to-back traumas of Vietnam and Watergate to offer Americans a soothing combination of honesty, humility, and quiet confidence. A great many political pundits, northern-bred, by and large, had some difficulty accepting the premise that a drawling Southern Baptist Sunday school teacher could actually run the country, but drawing heavily on the support of black voters, Carter managed to hold off a late surge by Republican opponent Gerald R. Ford and become the first Georgian ever to hold the presidency.

In Georgia and across the South generally, Carter's victory triggered a massive outpouring of what might only be called "redneck euphoria." (According to Blount, the simple realization that "a Southern Baptist, simple-talking, peanut-warehousing, grit-eating 'Eyetalian'-saying Cracker" had somehow managed to win the Democratic presidential nomination led his brother-in-law, Gerald — just returned from teaching English in England — to exclaim, "We ain't trash no more!") Meanwhile, a host of national publications joined the Dixie love feast, seizing on Carter's election to celebrate "the South as New America." For a brief period "redneck chic" was definitely in vogue as reporters descended on Carter's Sumter County home of Plains, lavishing much of their attention on the wit and wisdom of his charming and strong-willed mother, Miss Lillian, and the antics of "first brother" Billy, a wise-cracking, beer-swilling, shoot-from-the-hip small-town character, who distinguished between rednecks and "good ole boys" by noting whether when riding around in their pickups drinking beer they threw their cans out the window or tossed them in the floor of the truck. With Rev. M. L. "Daddy" King Sr. opening the day with a prayer service at the Lincoln Memorial, Carter's inauguration was replete with sweetness and irony, all of it suggesting in one way or another Georgia's emergence as both symbol and substance of a united and ascendant South.

As is usually the case, however, what seemed too good to be true actually was. The fascination with Georgia accents faded quickly as did amusement with Billy's increasingly drunken and boorish antics. Washington insiders complained about a surfeit of Georgians in their midst, though no such laments had seemed to go up when previous administrations had been saturated with White House personnel from Massachusetts or California. The teetotaling and unpretentious Carters were soon under fire for lacking "class," and runaway inflation and soaring interest rates took their toll beyond the beltway as well. When, in true Southern Baptist fashion, Carter lectured the American people about the need to lower their expectations, he breached the fine line between preaching and meddling for a generation steeped in instant gratification and self-indulgence. His inability to deal effectively with the Iranian hostage crisis sealed his bitter fate as he lost the presidency to Ronald Reagan, whose saber rattling and posturing for the religious right made him sound (save for the drawl) more southern than Carter. Many Georgians still express dismay at Carter's performance as president, but since his return to private life, his role as an international negotiator for peace, his profound faith in democracy and human rights, and his equally profound commitment to relieving human misery on a global scale have won him unequivocal respect across the nation and around the world. In 2002 he followed in the footsteps of Rev. Martin Luther King Jr. by becoming Georgia's second recipient of the Nobel Peace Prize. In his acceptance speech, Carter noted King's dream that in Georgia "the sons of former slaves and the sons of former slaveowners will be able to sit down together at a table of brotherhood" and suggested that "in a symbolic but very genuine way, at least involving two Georgians, it is coming true in Oslo today."

PROGRESS: FOR SOME MORE THAN OTHERS

For a time, at least, Georgia's barriers to black advancement seemed easier to transcend than the obstacles confronting women. Georgia had been the first state to reject the Nineteenth Amendment granting women's suffrage, and it became one of fifteen states that refused to ratify the equal rights amendment after it had been approved by Congress in 1972. Although World War II had drawn large numbers of Georgia women into the factory for the first time, more than ten thousand of them into Marietta's Bell Bomber plant alone, many of these had returned to domestic pursuits after the war. Still, with the heavy concentration of manufacturing employment in apparel and textiles, women nonetheless made up almost a third of Georgia's industrial workforce by 1950. In the early post–World War II years, these women typically continued to be farm wives, still responsible for all the cooking and chores they had handled before they began to work an eight-hour shift in a cotton mill or garment plant. In 1970 nearly 60 percent of the white women in the state's workforce were either textile and apparel operatives or secretaries and clerks. Meanwhile, black women were concentrated in service jobs, either in private homes or in restaurants and motels, although they were beginning to move into the mills as better jobs lured white women away. Professional opportunities for women of any color consisted largely of teaching and nursing, however, and average earnings for all female workers amounted to only around 60 percent of what males received.

Women who sought greater freedom and opportunity without leaving the state generally headed to Atlanta. In 1950 the portion of females in the workforce was more than a third higher in the Georgia capital than in the state at large. By 1960 the gap had narrowed to 14 percent, but it remained fairly stable for the next twenty years before narrowing dramatically in the 1980s. By that time, the Atlanta area had long been an irresistibly seductive land of opportunity for large numbers of Georgians regardless of gender or race. By the end of the 1980s, the eighteen counties of the Atlanta metropolitan area accounted for 44 percent of the state's population, 48 percent of its jobs, and 52 percent of its personal income. In 1994, *Fortune* magazine selected Atlanta as the world's fourth-best city for "global" business operations. "Even in Baghdad they know Atlanta," the writer gushed.

News such as this and the report that the Atlanta metro area led the nation in job creation in 1993 reinforced the impression of thoroughgoing prosperity within as well as around the Georgia capital. In reality, if, as some insisted, there were "two Georgias," then there were also "two Atlantas," one marked by suburban affluence and the other by inner-city poverty. In fact, the state's most startling contrasts in wealth and income could be found within fifteen miles of each other in Fulton County. North of the city in the Dunwoody Country Club area, family incomes typically exceeded $150,000 by 1990, while downtown in the housing projects around Spelman and Morehouse colleges, 94 of every 100 residents lived below the poverty level. Overall, 27 percent of the residents of the city of Atlanta fell into the latter category, giving the South's ostensibly most prosperous city the distinction of also being the nation's ninth poorest with a poverty rate only slightly higher than that of Mississippi, the South's and the nation's most economically deprived state. As incomes soared in fast-growing outlying counties like Cobb and Gwinnett, nearly half of downtown Atlanta's black neighborhoods actually grew poorer during the 1980s.

A COUNTRYSIDE TRANSFORMED

Although economic growth proceeded at a more modest pace outside metro Atlanta, it brought some notable changes to the countryside nonetheless. For thousands of rural Georgians happy to have jobs — even jobs that paid considerably less than those of their metropolitan cousins — the symbol of progress became not the skyscraper or the suburban split-level but the satellite dish beside the new double-wide mobile home. Wide or narrow, mobile homes accounted for at least 25 percent of the housing units in sixty-five counties in 1990. Modular living and multichannel viewing seemed to carry revolutionary sociological implications, but Georgians quickly clasped these innovations to their cultural bosoms. Those who did not get enough fire and brimstone, pulpit-thumping preaching on Sunday could find it in abundance on any day and at any hour on their satellite receivers. Those inclined to more hedonistic amusements insisted with mock seriousness that they could tell by the angle of a friend's dish whether he was watching the Playboy channel. (This particular jest was ultimately rendered obsolete by advances in the same technology that spawned it as large, rotatable antennas gave way to small, stationary dishes that made it impossible to distinguish one viewer's predilections from another's.) At the same time, the double-wide quickly entered local legend and musical lore as well. A popular ditty among country music fans celebrated the charms of the "queen of my double-wide trailer."

Double-wide trailers were readily associated with young couples coping with the potentially destructive stresses of making ends meet. They were also notoriously susceptible to destruction by the frequent tornadoes that swept across Georgia. Hence a popular joke went something like this: "What do a tornado and a South Georgia divorcee have in common? . . . Sooner or later, they're both gonna get the double-wide."

Across rural and small-town Georgia, the process of change was sometimes rapid and sweeping and other times uneven and slow but always fascinating. As in the rest of the southern states, an industrial economy came late to Georgia, the consequence being that manufacturing plants could take simultaneous advantage of rural electrification and farm mechanization by fanning out across the countryside to employ the cheap labor rendered even more expendable by the transformation of the farm economy. If casual observers were often struck by how rural Georgia seemed, closer observers were even more surprised by the number of industrial plants that dotted the rural landscape. Georgia led the nation in carpet production by the 1990s, and most of the carpet-manufacturing facilities were concentrated in mountainous Northwest

Georgia. As a result, Murray County, which was virtually saturated with carpet plants, enjoyed the distinction of being the nation's most industrialized county in terms of the portion of the labor force (62 percent) employed in manufacturing. Eleven other nonmetropolitan Georgia counties joined Murray on the list of the nation's top seventy-five counties in this category.

The carpet industry actually had its beginnings in Northwest Georgia in the manufacture of tufted textiles, particularly bedspreads, sewn by women working from home as independent seamstresses. After World War II, when the emergence of carpet making required workers with special tufting skills, the women of Murray, Whitfield, and surrounding counties moved into the factories. In such rural areas where textile and garment plants sought a predominantly female work force, the traditional gender hierarchy clearly took a hit, especially as the husbands of many of these women were forced to admit that small-scale farming had effectively played out. Since there were typically few jobs for them in the local "sewing plants," such men soon became known as "go-getters," because their principal daily responsibility was transporting their bread-winning (and still bread-making) wives to work. As 4:30 approached each afternoon, many a rural Georgia husband would rise from his seat on a Coca-Cola crate at the crossroads store, check his watch, and say, "Well, boys, I got to go get 'er."

There was considerable sacrifice in masculine dignity involved in becoming a "go-getter," and as the impossibility of making any sort of decent living as a small farmer became inescapably apparent, most farm men were forced to accept whatever industrial employment they could find. In doing so, they reclaimed their role as the family's principal breadwinner, but for many, giving up on the land was something akin to giving up on themselves. Having reached this point in his early fifties, my father put our farm in the Soil Bank Program, which paid us more to simply let it lie fallow than anyone could remember making when we had farmed it. When he finally found a job in a local shock-absorber plant, I thought we were rich. For the first time ever, I had an allowance, and we were able to trade in our woefully embarrassing (to me, at least) 1948 Chevrolet for a very respectable 1956 Ford. In the material and financial sense, we were clearly much better off than we had ever been. Yet though my father was doing a good job as a provider, he did so at considerable sacrifice of status, and, I'm afraid, self-respect. He had cherished the independence of farming in a way that all who are born and bred to it seem to, and the idea of submitting to the whistle and the regimen of the factory filled his heart with dread. His morning good-byes to us were protracted and almost pathetic, as if he were journeying to an alien and hostile place from which he might not return. He lived for the weekends, which he devoted in large measure to tending his garden, the only activity that seemed to give him any satisfaction. As I recall him now, I reel back past the slump-shouldered figure, carrying the unfamiliar lunch pail and shuffling reluctantly toward his job at "the plant," to recall the jaunty pose he always adopted as, Tampa Nugget clenched between his teeth, he steered his John Deere tractor and Allis Chalmers combine across the fields he knew and loved so well.

Georgia novelist Erskine Caldwell had captured the passion for the land that gripped Georgians of both races in the person of *Tobacco Road* protagonist Jeeter Lester, who, for all his depravity, sought incessantly to borrow a mule and secure the credit necessary to buy the seed and the guano he needed to plant one more cotton crop. This urge was particularly strong in the spring when others were preparing to plant their crops, because "the smell of newly turned earth, that others were never conscious of, reached Jeeter's nostrils with a more pungent odor than anyone else could ever detect in the air. That made him want to go out right away and burn over the old cotton fields and plant a crop."

Though his efforts to grow one more cotton crop came to naught, Jeeter refused to give up, knowing that his identity — his very man-hood — was tied to breaking the land and making it grow cotton. When advised repeatedly to seek work in a nearby cotton mill, Jeeter refused, despite his poverty, to exchange his soul for a steady paycheck: "No! By God and Jesus, no! . . . That's one thing I ain't going to do! The

Lord made the land, and He put me here to raise crops on it. . . . The land was where I was put at the start, and it's where I'm going to be at the end."

Coming of age during rural Georgia's transformation from agriculture to industry, I was witness to a number of changes that signaled the waning of a way of life. One of these involved revival meetings that had traditionally been staged in late summer so as to coincide with "laying-by time" (the point when the cotton was too large to cultivate, and therefore farmers could withdraw from their fields and wait for the bolls to mature and open for picking). As industrial employment increased, this schedule was maintained, but most churches gave up on the traditional two-a-day services, since only the older members and children were free to come to church on weekday mornings and fewer women were at home to "feed the preacher" his midday meal. With women flocking into factories, at church suppers and the legendary dinners-on-the-ground (remember that in those days "dinner" meant the midday meal), the onset of industrialization manifested itself in the appearance of various kinds of sandwiches prepared in haste using canned pineapple, processed pimento cheese, and fast-blackening bananas spread on store-bought "loaf bread." Even the traditional staple, the ham biscuit, lost much of its cultural authenticity with the appearance of that most abominable of all modern culinary innovations, the canned biscuit.

A LITERARY AWAKENING

The economic and demographic changes that swept across Georgia in the years after the Great Depression not only manifested themselves in significant changes in lifestyles and popular culture but formed the backdrop for a literary awakening as well. Writing in 1917, a contemptuous H. L. Mencken described Georgia as a literary wasteland where "intellectual stimulation" was "utterly lacking" and insisted that "in thirty years it has not produced a single idea." Georgians were not inclined to suffer such insults in silence. Mencken received repeated floggings on the editorial pages of dozens of Georgia newspapers, and he was also swamped with hate mail from outraged Georgians who were convinced that he surely must have leapt to his critical conclusions without reviewing Georgia's considerable contributions to American culture. They reminded Mencken and his equally condescending colleagues that Newton County, Georgia, was the home of the first Boy's Corn Club in the South and that Mrs. F. R. Goulding of Savannah was the first to suggest setting Heber's "From Greenland's Icy Mountains" to music. Another writer called Mencken's attention to "Georgia's brilliant poet," Frank L. Stanton (whose most famous composition was entitled "Mighty Lak' a Rose").

If these responses seemed only to confirm Mencken's put-downs, the painful truth was that Georgians leapt to the defense of the literary reputation of their beloved state with precious little ammo at their disposal. They might have cited the writings of Sidney Lanier, whose concern for preserving the land and the South as a region where people lived on the land put him at odds with Henry Grady's late-nineteenth-century New South crusade and made him the spiritual ancestor of the Nashville Agrarians, who attacked industrialism in the 1920s. Yet as an essayist and a poet, Lanier never made it to the big time. Critics complained of his sentimentality and his obsession with rhythm and rhyme, and his primary audience became several generations of Georgia school children who were compelled to memorize either his "Song of the Chattahoochee":

> Out of the hills of Habersham,
> Down the valleys of Hall,
> I hurry amain to reach the plain,
> Run the rapid and leap the fall. . . .

or "The Marshes of Glynn":

> As the marsh-hen secretly builds on the watery sod,
> Behold I will build me a nest on the greatness of God.

Otherwise, the would-be defenders of Georgia's literary virtue could turn only to Joel Chandler Harris, respected today as an excellent local colorist who made a major contribution by collecting and preserving black folklore in his "Uncle Remus" tales. To a disdainful Mencken, however, this latter activity made Harris "little more than an amanuensis for the local blacks." Always quick to judge and merciless when he did, Mencken scoffed that when Harris began to write on his own "as a white man . . . he swiftly subsided into the fifth rank."

If Georgians' emotional attacks only gave the hateful Mencken an even bigger chuckle at their state's expense, in just a few years the laugh would be on him, for, save perhaps for Mississippi, no state contributed more richly than Georgia to the post–World War I regional literary awakening that we now know as the Southern Literary Renaissance. In its complexity and diversity, the literature of modern Georgia provided an accurate reflection of the rapidly evolving society from which it flowed. Georgia's new breed of writers often seemed obsessed with debunking the myth of the glorious Old South and exposing the evils of the status quo, yet — like the citizenry at large — they were also more than a little ambivalent about the changes they could already see and apprehensive about a future they could only imagine.

Best known for his 1930s novels *God's Little Acre* and *Tobacco Road*, Erskine Caldwell actually authored or coauthored sixty books with combined sales topping eighty million copies. Caldwell was Georgia's best-selling writer, but owing to his often sensational depictions of southern poor white depravity, he was not its most popular one. That designation for white Georgians, at least, belonged to Caldwell's contemporary, Margaret Mitchell. Born in 1900, Margaret Munnerlyn "Peggy" Mitchell spent a year at Smith College before returning home to "keep house" for her widowed father. After a year on the debutante scene in Atlanta, she became a reporter for the *Atlanta Journal*. Mitchell quickly became the talk of polite society as she established a reputation for salty language and fast living. Her credentials in the latter category derived in no small part from an infamous Apache dance routine that she performed at a charity ball in 1921. In 1922 Mitchell married Berrien K. "Red" Upshaw, a former University of Georgia football player. The handsome and flamboyant Upshaw had credentials as a less-than-solid citizen that reportedly included a stint as a bootlegger running illicit alcohol between the Georgia mountains and Atlanta. The Mitchell-Upshaw union lasted but a few tumultuous months, and in 1925 she married the much more sedate John Marsh, an advertising executive for the Georgia Power Company. The mishap-prone victim of several automobile accidents, Mitchell began writing the novel that would become *Gone with the Wind* while recuperating from a broken ankle. Dubious of its merit, she did not submit it to an editor for several years.

Mitchell insisted that she never intended that Scarlett O'Hara become the heroine of her novel, but as the dominant character in the book, the nervy and resourceful Scarlett emerged as just that. Mitchell claimed that she deplored Scarlett's selfishness and vulgarity, but there seems to have been more than a little of Peggy in the character of Scarlett. As a young girl, Mitchell had been as flirtatious and manipulative as they came; toying with men, she treaded seductively along a fine line whereon she encouraged their ardor and abruptly spurned their advances. In fact, as she admitted, she harbored a deep-seated fascination with sexually aggressive males: "I used to have an elegant time in my early youth . . . by giving a life like imitation of a modern young woman whose blistering passions were only held in check by an iron control. It frequently succeeded so well that all thoughts of seduction were tabled and rape became more to the point."

As a novel and even more so as a movie, *Gone with the Wind* became the absolute embodiment of the romantic "moonlight-and-magnolias" vision of the Old South. Mitchell found this both ironic and disturbing, for she had seen her book as a frontal assault on the Old South myth. "I certainly had no intention of writing about cavaliers," she wrote, adding, "Since my novel was published, I have been embarrassed on many occasions by finding myself included among writers who pictured the South as a land of white-columned mansions whose wealthy owners had thousands of slaves and drank thousands of juleps. I have been surprised, too, for North Georgia certainly was no such country — if it ever existed anywhere — and I took great pains to describe North Georgia as it was. But people believe what they like to believe and the mythical Old South has too strong a hold on their imaginations to be altered by the mere reading of a 1,037 page book."

Whatever Mitchell's intentions, thanks to her novel and the subsequent film, countless readers and viewers in the United States and all over the world were reinforced in their vision of an Old South where planters ruled benignly over their grateful and happy slaves. If there was considerable irony in Margaret Mitchell's unwitting association with an Old South myth she set out to debunk, there was much deeper irony in the career of another well-known Georgia writer, Frank Yerby of Augusta. An African American, Yerby studied at Paine College, Fisk University, and the University of Chicago and during the 1940s wrote several short stories built around racial themes. Critics appreciated this work, but Yerby went on to fame and considerable fortune by largely ignoring such concerns in most of his later work. Published in 1946, Yerby's *The Foxes of Harrow* sold over two million copies, and in the two decades that followed, Yerby was the dominant figure in the southern romance genre. Solidly researched and vividly detailed, Yerby's novels were targeted for a white female audience, many of whom apparently never realized that their favorite author was black. And why should they? As Jack T. Kirby observed, "Yerby's South was Margaret Mitchell's without Mammy. There are baronial estates supporting fabulous wealth, decadent aristocrats and frontier swashbucklers on the make, pallid indoor belles and flushed hellions a la Scarlett or Jezebel. . . . Blacks figure as characters hardly at all."

Though not nearly as successful commercially as Caldwell, Mitchell, or Yerby, Flannery O'Connor now ranks as Georgia's most critically acclaimed writer of fiction. Like Lillian Smith and fellow Georgian Carson McCullers, O'Connor often shocked her readers. A Roman

Catholic, she viewed with critical detachment the entrenched, obsessive, and, in her portrayals, often hypocritical and hollow devotion of her fellow southerners to fundamentalist Protestantism. Yet if O'Connor was frustrated with most of the inhabitants of her "Christ-haunted" region, she was no more sympathetic to liberal critics and antagonists who indulged their own vanity, preached their own gospel of relativism, and denied the existence of original sin. In *Wise Blood*, O'Connor's Hazel Motes even attempts to establish "the Church without Christ" in a dilapidated automobile that ends up covered with kudzu in a Georgia pasture. In one of her most famous short stories, "A Good Man Is Hard to Find," a daffy old matron leads her entire family to destruction at the hands of "the Misfit," a cold-blooded killer, who blames his troubles on Jesus Christ and defines pleasure solely in terms of the harm he can inflict on others. When, in the course of trying to save her own life, the old lady stops urging him to seek Jesus and tries to embrace him as one of her own children, he shoots her at point-blank range and offers a fitting inscription for her tombstone, observing that "she would of been a good woman, if it had been somebody there to shoot her every minute of her life."

Like her contemporaries, O'Connor was witness to a rapidly accelerating process of change that brought the destabilizing and depersonalizing effects of industrialization and agricultural mechanization to the rural and small-town South. In "The Displaced Person," O'Connor told the story of a Polish immigrant, Mr. Guizac, who finds work as a hired hand on a rundown Georgia farm and revitalizes it through his energy, industriousness, and mechanical expertise. Yet, for all the economic benefits he brings, Guizac is also infected with alien values. His employer, Mrs. McIntyre, is impressed by Guizac's accomplishments and happy with the potential profits his efforts may reap for her, but she also worries that Guizac is a stranger to the society and culture in which he lives. Her fears are confirmed when she learns that he plans to get a female cousin into the United States by betrothing her to a local black man, and in the story's startling conclusion, she looks on silently, offering no warning, as the unsuspecting Guizac is flattened by a runaway tractor.

O'Connor specialized in calling attention to the spiritual shortcomings of her characters, but unlike Lillian Smith, she was no crusader for change. In fact, some of her most appreciative readers were distressed with her coolness toward the civil rights movement and several of its leaders. O'Connor remained dubious of the presumption of northern superiority and made no secret of her suspicion of "all those who come from afar with moral energy that increases in direct proportion to the distance from home." While southern liberals worked assiduously to bring the South into the American mainstream, O'Connor was concerned not by "the fact that the South is alienated from the rest of the country but by the fact that it is not alienated enough, that every day we are getting more and more like the rest of the country, that we are being forced out, not only of our many sins but of our few virtues."

Known for the Gothic settings and grotesque characters she created, Flannery O'Connor had a worthy successor in Harry Crews. Born to a poor white family in Bacon County, "the worst hookworm and rickets part of Georgia," as he called it, Crews set much of his fiction in the scrub pine, sandy-soil areas of South Georgia or North Florida. His first novel, *The Gospel Singer*, was especially evocative of O'Connor's fascination with the hypocrisy of Bible Belt fundamentalism, and Crews explained in the epigraph to his book that "men to whom God is dead worship one another."

Concerned with alienation of southerners from a regional society and culture rapidly losing its identity and meaning, Crews set his 1976 novel, *Feast of Snakes*, in a miserable South Georgia town whose traditional rattlesnake roundup has degenerated into a tourist attraction. Crews's central character, Joe Lon Mackey, is a former high school gridiron star who always had his way with the cheerleaders but never mastered the fine arts of reading and writing. Denied the opportunity to pursue collegiate stardom, he finds himself trapped in a miserable, frustrated existence, living in a mobile home with a wife with rotten teeth and two smelly infants for whom he feels little affection. After a torrid sexual encounter with his old girlfriend, Berenice, who has gone on to fame as a baton twirler at the University of Georgia, Joe Lon eventually goes on a homicidal shooting spree and is thrown by an angry mob into a pit full of writhing reptiles. As the novel closes, he struggles to his feet with snakes hanging from his face.

Like so many contemporary writers, poet and novelist James Dickey dealt with the transformation of southern life in his novel *Deliverance*. When Dickey's four suburbia-softened protagonists seek to reinvigorate themselves through the conquest of a wild North Georgia river, they encounter a group of murderous and perverted mountain men who only make the struggle with the river all the more desperate and terrible. The three who survive emerge feeling neither heroic nor, in any perceptible sense, better for their ordeal.

Historian David R. Goldfield noted that the civil rights movement went a long way toward removing "the public obsession with race," thereby allowing southern "whites to regain contact with other cultural elements such as past, place, and manners." Goldfield might have said the same for southern blacks, especially southern black writers. Whereas Richard Wright and Ralph Ellison struggled with a world dominated by the pervasive and confining realities of color, their successors felt less urgently the need to analyze the effects of white antagonism. Hence they could focus on the strengths and soft spots, complexities and contradictions of African American life.

Born, like Harry Crews, to a sharecropper family, Alice Walker grew up near Eatonton, studied at Spelman and Sarah Lawrence, and worked as a civil rights activist in Mississippi during the 1960s. Yet Walker's fiction was distinguished by her desire to look beyond (though certainly not ignore) white oppression and explore themes of community, identity, and gender in her writing. Walker had journeyed to Africa in search of her proverbial "roots," and in her short story "Everyday Use," a young woman named Dee, who, thanks to having her African consciousness raised, now calls herself Wangero, comes home to visit her impoverished mother. Wangero begs her mother to give her some handmade quilts that are already promised to Maggie, her disfigured and inarticulate sister, who is about to marry an ignorant, mossy-toothed country black man. Having refused the offer of these "old-fashioned" quilts when she went away to college, Wangero now wants them to hang on display. "Maggie can't appreciate those quilts!" she argues with unintended irony. "She'd probably be backward enough to put them to everyday use."

In *The Color Purple*, Walker went on to explore male-female and female-female relationships within the black family and community, stressing the strength and courage of her female characters as they struggled for fulfillment in a world dominated not just by whites but by males as well. More recently, Tina McElroy Ansa offered an irreverent look at the cult of matriarchy in *Ugly Ways*, a novel that reaches a riotous conclusion as the ever-combative Lovejoy sisters fall to scuffling at the funeral home, accidentally dump their mother's corpse on the floor, and proceed to deliver a series of recitations on her shortcomings as a parent.

"JUST AN OLD SWEET SONG . . ."

The role of Georgians in creating a new regional persona went well beyond the written page. Georgia performers contributed heavily to new musical traditions that were rich, complex, and ultimately intertwined in a process of cultural interaction and commercialization that produced a number of fascinating and distinctive musical styles. One of Georgia's musical pioneers was Fiddlin' John Carson, a major figure in the formative years of country music. Having gained notoriety for his incessant playing of the incendiary "Ballad of Little Mary Phagan" from the Marietta courthouse steps on the day Leo Frank was lynched, Carson seemed very much rooted in Cash's South. Founded in an indigenous folk and gospel tradition and recorded in 1923, his version of "Little Log Cabin in the Lane" became the first commercially successful "country" recording. Yet Carson's record sales depended ultimately on his ability to create new material, and he became one of country music's first professional composers. Carson's version of "There Ain't No Bugs on Me" commented on the Ku Klux Klan and the evolution controversy and even took an irreverent poke at famous evangelist Billy Sunday, noting that Sunday's church was always full because the people came "from miles around to hear him shoot the bull."

On the other side of the color line, Georgia not only produced blues legends Blind Willie McTell and Gertrude "Ma" Rainey, but Villa Rica's Thomas A. Dorsey, the son of a Baptist minister, who wrote and performed a number of explicitly raunchy blues tunes only to turn away from this sinful life to become a prominent gospel composer. Among his five hundred compositions, Dorsey listed hymns such as "Take My Hand, Precious Lord," and "There Will Be Peace in the Valley," a song made famous by Red Foley and recorded by a host of other white performers as well. The conflicts between the secular and spiritual also manifested themselves in a number of other Georgia performers. Save perhaps for the incomparably outrageous Jerry Lee Lewis, no southern musician seemed more torn between his hedonist impulses and puritan upbringing than Macon's Little Richard Penniman. A rock 'n' roll pioneer, Little Richard began his career in blues clubs and went on to record sexually charged tunes such as "Tutti Frutti" and "Good Golly, Miss Molly" only to turn to preaching and Bible study and then proceed to bounce back and forth between the Lord's work and the Devil's music. Meanwhile, Augusta's James Brown employed a host of gospel-derived techniques as he claimed the title "Godfather of Soul," and Macon's Otis Redding also achieved legendary status in the same genre. Finally, Albany native Ray Charles produced an astounding blend of the sacred and the secular in songs such as "I Got a Woman" and "What I Say" and went on to make himself all but synonymous with Hoagy

Carmichael's immortal "Georgia." While early white rock 'n' rollers succeeded in adapting their country and gospel heritage to the heavy beat of rhythm and blues, Charles was one of the few black performers who reciprocated by recording an album of country favorites that sold over 3 million copies. As the blues, gospel, and country styles moved toward the intersection that would yield the revolutionary musical hybrid known as rock 'n' roll, they reflected a pattern of change, both broad and deep, encompassing urbanization, industrialization, and the emergence of a youth culture distinguished by a considerably less rigid moral code than the one offered them by their parents.

Country music chronicled this process of change with particular candor. For nineteen-year-old Decatur native Bill Anderson, the view from the top of the hotel in then-tiny Commerce sufficed as inspiration for "City Lights," a song in which he imaginatively surveys a beckoning "Great White Way" only to reject the big city's allure when he reaches the conclusion that he "just can't say 'I love you' to a street of city lights." Anderson later offered a nostalgic reconsideration of the good old days when times were bad in his hit song "Po' Folks," which told of a family who were such a "hungry bunch" that even a wolf would not approach their front door without "a picnic lunch." Anderson's "Po' Folks" had something money couldn't buy, however, and instead of shivering from the cold or complaining about hunger, they simply "patched the cracks and set the table with love."

Several country tunes have provided inspiration for movies, but Anderson's "Po' Folks" may have been the only one ever to launch a restaurant chain. Featuring mass-produced "home-cooked" vittles washed down by mason jars full of iced tea, Anderson's PoFolks restaurants spawned a host of imitators by catering to those who, now that they no longer had to subsist on them, found an occasional meal of cornbread, beans, and greens an appealing way to make a brief visit to the simple pleasures of the past without returning to its hardships and trials on a permanent basis.

With Georgia changing more rapidly by the minute, nostalgia was in vogue not just in country music and foodways, but in literary and journalistic circles as well. In his 1976 novel, *The Year the Lights Came On*, Terry Kay recalled how the coming of electricity to rural Georgia helped to break down the social barriers between town and country but did so only at the cost of the "intangible security people have always enjoyed in isolation." In Kay's novel, rural electrification begins a process that television and air conditioning would subsequently accelerate, as a people accustomed to constant contact with nature suddenly began to spend more time indoors, developing, as Kay put it, "pretensions about the sophistication of having electricity."

In the course of telling his tale, Kay offered many a familiar vignette from small-town Georgia life, especially in his description of Rev. Bartholomew R. Bytheway's "Speaking-In-Tongues Traveling Tent Tabernacle revival" and the dramatic spiritual transformation of one Laron Crook, whose conversion "made St. Paul's experience on the road to Damascus seem like a migraine headache in comparison."

Elsewhere, Olive Ann Burns's *Cold Sassy Tree* told the story of a young man's coming of age in a small Georgia village modeled on the town of Commerce (which, ironically, had been the "big city" model for Bill Anderson's "City Lights"), and no writer better captured the spirit and rhythm of rural and small-town life in Georgia than Fayetteville physician and author Ferrol Sams Jr. In *Run with the Horsemen*, Sams displayed his considerable talents as a storyteller. One of his favorite characters was Mr. Lum Thornton, who lived at the poor farm but hung out at the barbershop:

One spring day Mr. Lum Thornton was rared back in his chair on the sidewalk, leaning against the light pole. His shirt sleeves were rolled halfway up his forearms and his collar unbuttoned at the neck. He had such thick, vibrant body hair that the boy was reminded in amazement of an animal pelt. . . . Up the sidewalk, regally erect and self-assured, on her way to call on Mrs. Babcock, swept the venerable and proud Miss Hess Meriwether. Pausing to acknowledge the nodding heads and respectfully murmured greetings of the group, her eyes fixed on the contented figure seated at the edge of the sidewalk. "My word, Lum," she said, "are you that hairy all over?"

The chair never budged. The eyes of the pauper met the eyes of the aristocrat. "Miss Hess," he drawled, "hit's a damn sight wuss'n that in spots."

By the early 1990s, South Georgia school teacher Bailey White had become National Public Radio's most popular commentator. A master storyteller, White captivated her urbane listeners with a skillful combination of down-home detail and sophisticated wit as she told of life with her offbeat though spunky and appealing mother and succeeded somehow in making Thomasville seem a somewhat cuddlier and sometimes wackier version of Garrison Keillor's Lake Woebegone slid South.

The propensity for wistful recollection was not peculiar to middle-class whites. Harry Crews's *A Childhood: The Biography of a Place* is perhaps the most touching and realistic memoir of poor-white life a southerner has produced. As a youth in Bacon County, Crews suffered through the loss of his father, a bout with polio, and an almost total immersion in scalding water. The night after his father was buried, all the meat disappeared from the family's smokehouse, stolen, according to Crews, by one of his father's friends. "It was a hard time in that land, and a lot of men did things for which they were ashamed and suffered for the rest of their lives," Crews explained. "The world that circumscribed the people I come from had so little margin for error, for bad luck, that when something went wrong, it almost always brought something else down with it. It was a world in which survival depended on raw courage born out of desperation and sustained by a lack of alternatives."

For all the hardships he and his people had known there, however,

Crews was by no means alienated from his South Georgia roots. He recalled with genuine affection the one-Saturday-a-month pilgrimages his family made to Alma, where around the square

> the dusty air would be heavy with the pleasant smell of mule dung and mule sweat. . . . Farmers were everywhere in small groups, talking and chewing, and bonneted women stood together trading recipes and news of children. . . . Sometimes I would have as much as a dime to spend on penny candy, but better than the taste of the candy was finding a telephone in a store and standing beside it until somebody used it. I never talked on one myself until I was almost grown, but I knew what a phone was, knew that a man's voice could be carried on a wire all the way across town. No film or play I have ever watched since has been as wonderful as the telephones I watched as a boy in Alma, Georgia.

Crews denied that he was "singing a sad song for the bad good old days, wishing he was back barefoot again traveling in wagons and struck dumb by the mystery of telephones. . . . What I am talking about here is a hard time in the shaping of the South, a necessary experience that made us the unique people we are." Such people are often the central characters in the poems and novels of Judson Mitcham, who captured both the wounding hardness of life at the margins of southern society and the healing softness that love, family, and memory can sometimes afford. Mitcham's first novel, *The Sweet Everlasting*, offered both tragedy and redemption in the story of a South Georgia sharecropper's son who marries a beautiful woman only to live most of his life in tragic separation from her; finally reunited with her in old age, he must come to terms with the Alzheimer's disease that prevents her from remembering him.

If it is surprising that writers like Crews and Mitcham have found such affirmation in the hardships and trials of Georgia's lower-class whites, it is surely no less striking to encounter a similar feeling in the novels of black writer Raymond Andrews, who grew up not far from Alice Walker in a sharecropping family near Madison, Georgia. Andrews dedicated his novel *Appalachee Red*, "To all those who [have] ever picked a boll of cotton, pulled a peach or gone to town on a Saturday afternoon." When Andrews decided to become a novelist, he determined to write, as he put it, "books about what I knew best: small town and rural black folks in the South and their relationship to both the land and their white neighbors. . . . My American roots (like those of most Afro-Americans) are southern rural. This particular land and the individuals who have lived and died on it are what my books are about." Although Andrews left Madison in 1949, he was clearly speaking from the heart when he explained many years later, "I still care for Madison and its people because I have many memories of the place and to me it will always be home."

For her part, although Alice Walker did not intend "to romanticize the Southern black country life," she actually seemed to express sympathy for her "Northern brothers" who "have never experienced the magnificent quiet of a summer day when the heat is intense and one is so very thirsty, as one moves across the dusty cotton fields, that one learns forever that water is the essence of all life. In the cities, it cannot be so clear to one that he is a creature of the earth, feeling the soil between the toes, smelling the dust thrown up by the rain, loving the earth so much that one longs to taste it and sometimes does."

Walker explained that she was "nostalgic" not for "lost poverty" but for "the solidarity and sharing a modest existence can sometimes bring." Yet, as she saw it, "No one could wish for a more advantageous heritage than that bequeathed to the black writer in the South: a compassion for the earth, a trust in humanity beyond our knowledge of evil, and an abiding love of justice."

Not all Georgia authors focused their wistful recollections on rural and small-town life. In *Peachtree Road*, Anne Rivers Siddons captured the heyday and described the demise of "Old Atlanta" society as reflected in the tragic disintegration of one affluent Buckhead family. Other observers saw little to celebrate in Atlanta's emergence as the quintessential symbol of a northernized South, lost for a second and final time to the Yankees — this time, ironically, through success rather than failure. Such was the perspective of Georgia-bred journalist Marshall Frady. Having made a name for himself primarily by showcasing the South's benightedness before the rest of the nation, Frady seemed to have received a massive injection of mellow by the mid-1970s. He recalled longingly a South that once seemed like "America's Corsica — an insular sunglowered latitude of swooning sentiment and sudden guttural violence, always half adaze in the past." That imagery was fading rapidly, however, as Frady surveyed a South teetering on the verge of being rendered "pastless, meaningless, and vague of identity." Below Atlanta, in the "aboriginal landscapes of *Gone with the Wind*," a horrified Frady encountered "a Santa Barbara gallery of pizza cottages and fish 'n' chips parlors, with a 'Tara Shopping Center' abruptly glaring out of fields of broom sage and jack pine."

Dismayed by this physical transformation, Frady was even more distressed by the "cultural lobotomy" evidenced by the disappearance of the "musky old demagogues" he had once loved to pillory and even the "chigger bitten tabernacle evangelists" whose "fierce tragic theologies" were little in evidence in suburban Atlanta, where bumper stickers read "PEOPLE OF DISTINCTION PREFER JESUS."

A LOTTERY FOR LEARNING

Such a restrained approach toward religion was far less common outside Atlanta, where Georgia's more conservative religious groups maintained a common vigil against certain secular encroachments, mustering their forces wherever and whenever the prospect of liberalized liquor laws or legalized gambling manifested itself. Zell Miller staked his 1990 gubernatorial campaign on a statewide lottery whose proceeds were to be dedicated to supporting education. Following legislative approval, the lottery question went to the voters on November 2, 1993, and attracted nearly as much attention as had the presidential clash between Bill Clinton and George H. W. Bush. Early polls showed majority support for the lottery, but a grassroots campaign against it gradually gained momentum as election day drew near. Organizers of GAAG (Georgia Alliance Against Gambling) did not rely solely on a religious message and attacked the lottery as a social evil rather than a sin, stressing its potential to accelerate the already alarming deterioration of the entire social fabric. Still, the opposition's campaign drew heavily on the support of Georgia's large church-going population, and many churches sported outdoor signs with antilottery slogans.

Returns showed that the late-developing opposition movement, which narrowly missed defeating the lottery proposal, drew heavily on the support of older, rural, church-going voters. On the other hand, support for the lottery was strongest in the state's urban counties, especially metropolitan Atlanta. The vote also broke along racial and class lines, with blacks supporting the measure by a two-to-one majority, while whites opposed it by a narrow margin. Jokesters labeled the lottery a ready-made "retirement plan" for rednecks, and in general, voters earning less than $30,000 per year had supported the lottery, while those earning more than $50,000 were more likely to oppose it. (First-year statistics on lottery participation revealed a similar pattern: Ticket purchasers were more likely to be black and less affluent.) Owing to heavy participation by buyers from neighboring states, the Georgia lottery set a first-year sales record, generating income equivalent to $160 for every resident of the state. (Fourteen years later, this figure had effectively doubled, with some lower income counties showing some of the highest lottery sales per capita.) Whatever the socioeconomic implications of the lottery itself, the revenues it generated were a boon for Georgia high school students. In addition to a variety of other programs, the lottery-driven HOPE (Helping Outstanding Pupils Educationally) program offered a four-year, full-tuition scholarship to attend any in-state public institution (and flat-rate tuition supplements at in-state private schools as well) to Georgia residents who earned a B average in high school and maintained the same average during their college careers.

If many Georgians at large hardly knew what to make of the lottery craze, they were alternately amused, bewildered, and sometimes angered by Atlanta's wholesale, hell-for-leather, heart-on-its-sleeve courtship of the 1996 Olympic Games. Atlanta's Olympic quest apparently began early in 1987 as the inspiration of Atlanta lawyer Billy Payne, who quickly enlisted the cooperation of Mayor Andrew Young and the city's chamber of commerce. There ensued a tedious and protracted process of courtship and competition in which Atlanta first bested Minneapolis–St. Paul as the preferred site of the U.S. Olympic Committee and then went on to confront four other competitors, including Athens (not the one just down the road, where the Bulldogs first played football in 1892, but the other one, where the first modern Olympics were held in 1896). Clearly Athens had both sentiment and symbolism going for it, but as the International Olympic Committee (IOC) proceeded through several votes, Atlanta gained increasing support, going over the top when Toronto was eliminated.

In addition to Payne, a key player in the Atlanta effort was the by-then former mayor Young, whose global connections from his days as U.S. ambassador to the United Nations stood him in good stead. There was considerable irony in observing a black southerner seeking African support for bringing the Olympics to a part of the world once notorious for its treatment of blacks. At any rate, on September 18, 1990, the announcement in Tokyo of Atlanta's selection elicited a riotous response from the 350 Georgians in attendance, while back in Atlanta, where it was six in the morning, approximately two thousand early risers watched the triumph via satellite amidst fluttering confetti, fireworks, and the release of twenty-five hundred balloons. Another huge celebration ensued that evening, followed by another the next morning.

Some more skeptical Georgians quickly grew tired of what became a marathon of self-congratulatory rhetoric and celebration, and those

eager to deflate Atlanta's balloon soon had their chance. Apparently selected without much consultation or market research, the 1996 Olympic
mascot "Whatizit" made its debut at the closing ceremonies of the 1992
Olympic Summer Games in Barcelona. To describe the debut as inaus-
picious would be an understatement of truly Olympic proportions. In
fact, only "unmitigated disaster" will suffice. A computer-generated and
wholly unendearing blue blob described by one commentator as "a bad
marriage of the Pillsbury Doughboy and the ugliest California Raisin,"
Whatizit met with "international derision." Among the homefolks,
the reception was even less cordial. Stunned members of the Atlanta
Committee for the Olympic Games (ACOG) insisted that the unlikely
mascot would grow on folks, but, their stiff upper lip notwithstanding,
they quickly launched a vigorous reassessment of what steps might be
taken to improve its marketability.

The result was a transformed Whatizit, cuddlier and more expressive,
sporting bigger feet, and bearing the nickname "Izzy." None of these
changes succeeded in pacifying Izzy/Whatizit's Georgia-based critics
who found him objectionable precisely because his regionally neutral
nerdiness seemed to stem from a desire to avoid any potential association of the Olympic Games with the South. One Georgian said, "I don't
get where he's coming from. I don't really see how it represents anything specific to Atlanta, to the South — to the country, even. It ought
to stand for something." Journalist Bert Roughton had other ideas as
to why some of the 57 percent of Atlantans polled in September 1993
found even the remodeled mascot objectionable: "Atlanta has been re-
inventing itself since it was reduced to ashes in the Civil War. . . . Maybe
that's why we all recoiled so much when we first laid eyes on Whatizit.
Maybe there was an uncomfortable recognition of something too familiar. Maybe it's just the ugly truth: Izzy is us."

The reimaging of Atlanta had long been a favorite local pastime, but
for all the efforts in this direction, as the 1990s unfolded, Atlantans
found themselves facing yet another identity crisis. Ironically, after selling their city as the site of the 1996 Summer Olympic Games, the city's

leadership wound up hiring a consultant (appropriately named Joel Babbit) to select a slogan describing what it was that they had actually sold. The search produced a flood of suggestions from the Henry Gradyesque "Atlanta: From Ashes to Axis" to the more candid but less inspiring "Atlanta: Not Bad for Georgia" to the also accurate but decidedly unpoetic "Watch Atlanta Transmogrify." Some warned that the great search for a slogan was likely to culminate in something along the lines of "Atlanta: A southern city of great hospitality where the weather is generally fair, the business climate is positive, a number of large buildings exist, and you can have fun at Underground." The eventual choice, "Atlanta. Come Celebrate Our Dream," was slick, sophisticated, and suitably bland, so much so that cynical observers suggested replacing it with "Atlanta: Where the South Stops" or "Atlanta: It's 'Atnalta' Spelled Backwards."

THE GREAT SYMBOL WAR

Of all the cultural ramifications of Atlanta's Olympic preparation, none provoked more verbal fireworks than the great state flag controversy. Adopted in 1799, Georgia's first state flag had consisted of the state's coat of arms on a field of blue. A new post-Reconstruction banner resembled the first flag of the Confederacy and featured a vertical blue strip and horizontal bands of red and white. The state's coat of arms was added to the flag in 1905. This banner flew over Georgia until 1956 when the legislature moved to incorporate the familiar Confederate battle flag into the state flag.

Defenders of this flag insisted that this modification was meant to honor Confederate soldiers, but it came at a time of confrontation, when the state's white political leaders were rallying to the cause of massive resistance to the 1954 *Brown v. Board of Education* decision and vowing last-ditch defiance of any and all desegregation efforts. Flag critics also pointed out that the day before the state House of Representatives approved the flag-change bill, it had passed by a vote of

179 to 1 the so-called Interposition Resolution, which declared the U.S. Supreme Court's school-integration decrees "null, void and of no effect" in Georgia. At the time, state representative Denmark Groover of Macon insisted that the new flag would "show that we in Georgia intend to uphold what we stood for, will stand for, and will fight for." James Mackay, a member of the 1956 legislature who had opposed adding the Confederate emblem to the state banner, was absolutely convinced that the intent of the bill's supporters was to affirm their support for segregation. He offered an analogy that anyone familiar with Georgia could readily understand: "There was only one reason for putting that flag on there. Like the gun rack in the back of a pickup, it telegraphs a message." (The association of the new state flag with the "southern way of life" was pervasive indeed. As an elementary and high school student in the late 1950s and early 1960s and as a high school teacher in the late 1960s, I recall that all classroom films acquired from the Georgia Department of Education began with a vivid shot of the state flag accompanied by a robust rendition of "Dixie.")

After the passions of the civil rights era had cooled somewhat, several individuals and groups launched assaults on the flag, the most notable coming in 1987 after a widely publicized incident in which white supremacists waving rebel flags attacked civil rights marchers in Forsyth County. Finally, in May 1992 Governor Zell Miller announced that he would support legislation to restore the pre-1956 flag and called the current flag "the last remaining vestige of days that are not only gone, but also days that we have no right to be proud of." Changing the flag would require "sheer guts," Miller acknowledged, but as the great-grandson of a Confederate soldier wounded at both Chancellorsville and Gettysburg, Miller found the flag a blemish on the state's image, and he added, "Frankly, I do give a damn."

Not surprisingly, with its large population of blacks and nonnative whites and its economic stake in projecting an image of enlightenment and harmony, the Atlanta area provided the strongest support for removing the Confederate battle flag from the state's official banner.

Meanwhile, supporters of the flag feared that the next step might be a sandblasting of Stone Mountain, especially after a black clergyman admitted that his dream was that someday folks would look up at the world's largest stone carving and say, "Who are those fellows?" Casual observers saw the flag controversy pitting the "fergit" crowd (composed of black activists and a smattering of white liberals) against the "fergit, hell" crowd (personified by the Sons of Confederate Veterans). In reality, the dispute was hardly that simple. Some polling data from Georgia showed that a majority of black respondents expressed no objection to keeping the state flag as it was. Meanwhile, though pro-flag partisans insisted that white southerners saw it as a memorial to their heroic Confederate forebears, a 1992 survey indicated that fewer than 20 percent of the southern whites polled could even claim such an ancestry. On the other hand, even white southerners of the liberal persuasion were sometimes a bit testy where the flag was concerned. When asked by an argumentative northerner why the South needed a flag when the North didn't have one, even the affable Roy Blount Jr. wanted to respond, "That's because the North isn't a place. . . . It's just a direction out of the South."

Though it often sparked heated and intemperate rhetoric on both sides, the assault on Confederate icons nonetheless raised intriguing questions about the appropriate symbols for a new southern identity. The same was true of the growing popularity among black tourists of memorials such as Atlanta's Martin Luther King Jr. Center for Nonviolent Social Change and Ebenezer Baptist Church and other civil rights landmarks elsewhere in the South.

Miller's move against the flag required considerable courage, but with polls consistently showing as much as 60 percent support for keeping the flag as it was, the outcome was hardly in doubt. By January 1994 the governor was facing reelection, and though he was no longer inclined to raise the flag issue, when someone else did, he simply conceded, "I gave it my best shot. I lost. . . . I lost that one big." Although he had conceded defeat on the flag, hard feelings on the issue contributed to a surprisingly close race in his bid for reelection that year, notwithstanding Miller's role in implementing Georgia's widely acclaimed HOPE Scholarship Program, which had won him bipartisan praise across the state and the nation.

Despite Miller's strategic retreat, the flag question simply refused to go away. Following the lead of the Atlanta City Council and the Fulton County Commission, the Atlanta–Fulton County Recreation Authority decided to remove the flag from Atlanta–Fulton County Stadium, the home of the Atlanta Braves at the time. At the Georgia Dome, where the Atlanta Falcons play, the presence of the flag sparked 1994 Super Bowl–day protests from various civil rights groups as well as a group of about fifty reporters who wore black arm bands and declined to enter the press box until after the national anthem had been played. Meanwhile, with the Olympics still two years away, the Hyatt, the Westin Peachtree Plaza, and other major downtown Atlanta hotels stopped flying the state flag, and Holiday Inn Worldwide asked its Georgia franchises to do the same. Other than angering a fair number of white Georgians, these decisions may have accomplished relatively little in the short run. In hindsight, however, they demonstrated quite forcefully that when corporate executives were forced to choose between symbols, the Confederate flag was no match for the dollar sign. From this point on, it should have been clear that the question of a new state flag was not one of whether but merely one of when.

OLYMPIC GEORGIA

As the countdown to the 1996 Olympics moved from months to weeks, it remained to be seen whether the Atlanta games would further divide Georgians along not just racial and ideological but geographical and class lines as well. The state flag issue had refused to go away, and a few days before the games began, ACOG officials announced that spectators would be prohibited from waving the Georgia flag at Olympic events. The ban on flags was general rather than specific, but vociferous criticism ensued, especially when it became apparent that some ACOG officials hoped to keep the controversial aspects of the South's past out of the eyes and minds of Olympic visitors. Though normally in great demand during the summer, Civil War reenactors were reportedly told to pitch their tents elsewhere, and some historic sites around Atlanta were not only consciously deemphasizing slavery as a part of their story but were even shying away from the use of the term "antebellum."

Yet for all the nay-saying — and there certainly was aplenty — as the time neared, communities throughout Georgia clearly began to buy into the Olympics and joined Atlanta in trying to get the Olympics to buy into them. Tiny villages anywhere within reasonable driving distance of Atlanta or any of the satellite Olympic venues were sprucing themselves up, festooning lazy courthouse squares with Olympic banners, and inviting scores of athletes from around the world to come and hone their competitive skills in the unfamiliar and un-Atlanta-like environs of small-town Georgia.

The financial returns on serving as an Olympic training site were easily exaggerated, but cultural enrichment was a most welcome by-product. Across Georgia international athletes were welcomed into local communities with surprisingly little regard for ideology, theology, or race. LaGrange played consummate host to Olympic athletes from Nigeria, and Decatur entertained visitors from Ireland, demonstrating hospitality by temporarily turning the second floor of the Dekalb County Courthouse into an Irish pub. Decatur had already established strong ties with Burkina Faso, and it also embraced the thirty-five-member Olympic delegation from that tiny African nation. To show their appreciation, some of the Burkinabe performed an elaborate seduction dance on the Decatur square. Hartwell welcomed the rowing team from Belarus, who, at a get-acquainted picnic, introduced the locals to the practice of downing shots of straight vodka, quickly rendering several of their hosts thick of tongue and wobbly of gait. In addition to Hartwell's effusive hospitality, the Belarussians were also overwhelmed by Georgia's awesome heat and humidity. At an autograph party on the town square, the amiable former cold war adversaries sweated profusely and sought a brief respite by taking seats at the base of Hart County's monument to the Confederate dead.

Concerns that ACOG officials wanted to sidestep or de-emphasize Atlanta's southernness faded somewhat when the long-awaited opening ceremonies provided a dazzling, surprisingly Dixiefied extravaganza complete with Gladys Knight's rendition of "Georgia" and a convoy of seriously tricked out pickup trucks. Likewise, the much-ballyhooed Centennial Olympic Park featured southern music and crafts and an exhibit on southern agriculture that boasted mechanical cows and chickens and, in a somewhat futuristic twist, a robotized emu as well. Meanwhile, though protests against the state flag continued throughout the games, they seemed to attract relatively little attention from Olympic visitors. Nor, we might note in passing, did the flag controversy appear to be much of a concern to the hundreds of exotic dancers who descended on the city as its forty-odd strip clubs announced plans to add new shifts and remain open around the clock during the games.

Journalists from near and far (especially far) had been warning for months that Atlanta could not "handle" the Olympics, and early transportation and communications problems within the Olympic organization elicited a flood of "we told you so's" from the press corps. Moreover, despite spending untold amounts of money in a frenzied down-to-the-wire effort to spruce up downtown, ACOG had subcontracted with a company that saturated the area with sidewalk vending booths, most of them offering the same grossly overpriced merchandise and all of them adding to the overall impression of a garish carnival. From the beginning, the vendors sent up a howl that they had been sold their own bill of goods about the volume of sales they could expect.

On the other hand, Centennial Park itself proved to be by far the most popular nonathletic attraction, drawing thousands each day to escape the heat in the official Olympic fountain or attend free outdoor concerts that lasted until the wee hours of the morning. It was in the wee hours of July 27 that Atlanta's Olympic experience suddenly turned tragic. Stern warnings about the need for tight security and the high potential for terrorist activity had begun to lose force as the games proceeded largely without incident — until a pipe bomb exploded at a Centennial Park concert and injured 110 people, contributed to the death by heart attack of a Turkish journalist, and killed Alice Hawthorne of Albany, who had brought her daughter to Atlanta to witness the Olympic celebration.

Somber Olympic officials assured stunned athletes and spectators that the games would go on. Former Atlanta mayor Andrew Young praised all whose determined response to the bombing "really demonstrated the Olympic spirit." Young also predicted that Atlanta would ultimately be "strengthened" by the crisis, as ACOG spin doctors treaded perilously close to conveying the impression that ACOG was using the tragedy to rally support for Atlanta and the Olympic Games. Centennial Park reopened with a memorial service for Alice Hawthorne, but the official reopening ceremony quickly took on the overtones of a giant celebration, and within minutes of its conclusion, visitors were forming huge lines to buy souvenirs and visit the commercial sites within the park.

Among Georgians at large, Hawthorne's death did not go unnoticed nor did the story of her accomplishments as a businessperson and mother. The outpouring of sympathy for her family came with a palpable sense of public outrage, however, and many Georgians, especially Atlantans, clearly took the bombing personally, to the point of embracing the Olympics more tightly and warmly than before. Defiant and determined, visitors in even greater numbers pressed back into Centennial Park. Meanwhile, realizing that the pre-Olympic doom-sayers' predictions of terrible traffic, no parking, and a generally not-worth-the-hassle scenario had for the most part failed to materialize, others began to venture out, simply seizing the chance to be a part of it all before it was too late. By the time Atlanta bid its three million visitors a hearty "Bye, y'all" on August 4, ticket sales for individual events stood at 8.6 million — more than had been sold at the two previous summer games at Seoul and Barcelona combined.

The Atlanta games had been the biggest and best attended in history, but were they the "greatest" yet? Not according to a tight-lipped Juan Antonio Samaranch, the naughty one-time Spanish fascist leader who headed the International Olympic Committee. After complaining about the commercialism surrounding the games, Samaranch would only describe them at the closing ceremonies as "most exceptional." This deliberate damnation by measured praise was a crushing blow to image-obsessed ACOG officials and Atlanta boosters of all sorts. Ever sensitive to negative perceptions, the *Atlanta Journal-Constitution* ran regular editorial excerpts from other newspapers under such headings as "What They're Saying About: Atlantans and Southerners" and "What They're Saying About: Atlanta's Commercial Heart." Throughout the games the attention that Atlanta's leaders devoted to the amount and nature of publicity their city received was nothing short of striking. Responding to Samaranch's snub, Atlantans were soon sporting bumper stickers declaring, "Frankly, Juan Antonio, We Don't Give a Damn!" Clever, but not totally convincing, this revision of Rhett Butler's famous retort was part plain old American boosterism and part reaffirmation of W. J. Cash's description of southerners as "a people moved by the histrionic urge to perform in splendor, and by the patriotic will to testify to faith in their land and to vindicate it before the world's opinion."

A hastily conducted post-Olympic survey showed that slightly more than half of the respondents gave Atlanta an A for its role as host of the games. (It is worth noting that among southerners 57 percent were ready to award the A as compared with 48 percent of those residing elsewhere in the nation.) Ironically, a comparison poll taken before and after the Olympics showed that the generally favorable perception of Atlanta as a trendy, progressive city seemed largely unaffected by its stint in the Olympic spotlight. Forced to give an up close assessment of Georgia's Olympic experience, one could readily observe that chagrined vendors (like the one who was left with eighty thousand Izzy coloring books on his hands) and scores of other unrealistic would-be profiteers considered it not just disappointing but disastrous. Meanwhile, journalists from around the world won few friends in Georgia when their initial, often legitimate complaints speedily degenerated into an incessant, redundant chorus of nitpicking and whining. Offsetting the negative reviews from the media, however, was the well-nigh inescapable conclusion that an overwhelming number of those who attended the games enjoyed the experience immensely and went home pleased and impressed. Finally, despite occasional insistences of, "Shoot, I'm as close to all that as I want to be" and complaints that it was time to shoo all the foreigners out of Georgia and get on with football season, it seemed clear enough that from Chickamauga to Camilla and throughout the far reaches of the state, in surprising numbers and to a surprising extent, the people of Georgia had, however gradually and grudgingly, claimed the 1996 Olympic Games as their own.

More than ten years later, it remained unclear whether the Olympic experience truly marked a watershed in Georgia's history or even Atlanta's. It did seem fair to conclude that the 1996 Atlanta Olympics may have fallen perhaps a wee bit shy of Billy Payne's prediction that they would go down as "the greatest peacetime event in the history of the world." However, one estimate placed the overall economic impact of the games in excess of five billion dollars, most of it concentrated in the Atlanta vicinity, of course. The Olympics, after all, had brought Turner Field and the twenty-one-acre Centennial Park and, despite criticism for uprooting lower-income residents, even some newer, safer, low-cost housing for downtown in addition to new dormitories and other facilities for both Georgia Tech and Georgia State University. On the other hand, even the Olympic infusion of cash had failed to get perpetually troubled Underground Atlanta out of its economic hole, and despite efforts to tie it to the games, the city's wildly successful Georgia Aquarium, which opened in 2005, was located near Centennial Park largely due to other considerations. Although most conceded that expectations of an Olympic windfall had been irrationally exuberant in the first place, at least one development official admitted that "we didn't get as much out of it as we could have or should have."

Tormented by the nagging sense that the games did not quite "sell" their city, Atlanta's indefatigable image-engineers were at it again by 2005, launching a fifteen-million-dollar "Brand Atlanta" campaign aimed at creating and marketing a "collective personality" for a city that had never had one and was growing more rambunctiously diverse every day. (As Roy Blount Jr. put it in 2007, "In the beginning Atlanta was without form and void, and still is.") Thus did the Olympic-inspired "Come Celebrate Our Dream" give way to "Every Day Is an Opening Day" and, for good measure, "The ATL," a controversial, hip-hoppish new anthem, all in the apparent interest of winning the acceptance and approval of even more people from even more places with even more money.

BOOM IN THE "'BURBS"

Regardless of what the Olympic experience may have done or failed to do to make the city of Atlanta itself more attractive, it clearly did nothing to dampen the explosive growth that was already pushing its suburban boundaries well into the distance long before the site for the 1996 games was announced. The 1990s brought impressive growth in some of Georgia's smaller metro areas, but none of these could match metropolitan Atlanta, which by 2000 was home to over half of Georgia's population and generated 60 percent of the state's personal income. After adding nearly nine hundred thousand residents between 2000 and 2006 alone, it surged past both Boston and Detroit to become the nation's ninth-largest metro area.

By 2007 the Atlanta Metropolitan Statistical Area, now encompassing twenty-eight counties stretching down to Pike on one end and up to Pickens on the other, had seen its population swell to five million, twice what it had been twenty years earlier, and an additional two million residents were expected by 2020. The area also boasted twenty-five Fortune 500 companies and was adding sixty to seventy thousand new jobs annually. Within the metro area, the once rural counties of Fayette and Forsyth sported median family incomes well in excess of $70,000, the highest in the state, with Cherokee, Henry, Paulding, Gwinnett, Coweta, and Cobb also ranking in the top ten.

Forsyth County's story was particularly intriguing. Despite its reputation as a rural "sundown county" (meaning blacks had once been advised unequivocally to leave Forsyth before nightfall), its population had grown by 67 percent in the 1970s. Notwithstanding a violent confrontation between civil rights marchers and Klansmen in 1987, Forsyth registered a nearly 60 percent population increase during the 1980s. Although only fourteen African Americans chose to live there in 1990, with the recently completed Georgia 400 funneling commuters back and forth to Atlanta, Forsyth's population expanded by an additional 123 percent over the next ten years, marking it as one of the nation's fastest growing counties. The result was a development explosion of predictably seismic proportions, which soon had the landscape erupting with pretentiously titled residential developments such as "Dressage" and "Olde Atlanta Club." Meanwhile, as residents of Shakerag and Frogtown watched in both bewilderment and amazement, the princely sport of polo made its debut in an area where possum hunting had not long before been the principal leisure-time pursuit.

Although most blacks continued to avoid Forsyth County, metropolitan Atlanta's African American population swelled by 459,000 during the 1990s alone, and it boasted seven of the nation's top ten counties in terms of black population growth. Roughly half the black families in both Henry and Gwinnett counties enjoyed incomes of more than $50,000 by 1999. In Fayette County, meanwhile, the portion of black families earning $50,000 or more a year had risen from 42 percent in 1989 to 74 percent ten years later when nearly a third of all its black families showed annual incomes in excess of $100,000. Black business leaders claimed the area had the nation's largest middle-class black population, and one new black resident of metropolitan Atlanta admitted,

"There are so many African Americans here who have made it or succeeded or gotten to that middle-class line. It's nice to see."

On the other hand, in Atlanta and Fulton County proper, the historic economic gap between blacks and whites not only persisted but widened in the 1990s and beyond. With a median income of $68,000 in 1999, Fulton County's white households were among the metro area's most affluent, but with the median income of black households at roughly $29,000, its black residents were generally even worse off relative to whites than they had been a decade earlier. Thus, while Fulton County boasted the state's highest overall per capita income in 2004, its poverty rate was also 22 percent above the state average. This disparity was only exacerbated by a trend toward returning to downtown Atlanta among relatively affluent whites seeking urban amenities without the hassle of commuting. As an additional consequence of this influx, the black share of Atlanta's population had actually fallen from 67 percent in 1990 to 59 percent by 2005, feeding fears among black Atlantans that their influence on local affairs might be slipping away.

OUT BEYOND THE BOOM

Black poverty seemed strangely out of place amid metro Atlanta's affluence, but it was a long-established fact of life in many of the state's rural counties. According to the 2000 census, 45 percent of black households in Clay County were surviving on less than $10,000 per year in 1999. In fifteen other counties, this figure was more than one-third. In all, there were eighty-two Georgia counties where more than 30 percent of the black population lived below the poverty line in 1999.

Nor was white poverty yet a thing of the past in Georgia as the twenty-first century unfolded, certainly not in the twenty counties where at least 15 percent of the white families were getting by on less than $10,000 per year. Manufacturing employment had actually grown at the rate of 4 percent statewide during the 1980s, but many Georgia communities were already being hit hard by plant closings, especially in the textile and apparel industries, which lost ninety-eight hundred jobs between 1989 and 1992 alone.

This latter trend accelerated throughout the 1990s and beyond as industrial mobility and the lure of even cheaper labor elsewhere on the planet registered in the disappearance of more than a hundred thousand manufacturing jobs between 1997 and 2006, with perhaps 60 percent of these coming in the textile and apparel industries. Small "sewing plants" had once been a fixture of many of Georgia's small-town economies, but by 2005 fewer than four thousand Georgians actually held production jobs in the state's apparel factories, where employment had fallen by an astonishing 85 percent since 1997 alone. Meanwhile, in retrospect, with 14 percent of its industrial workers belonging to labor organizations, the Georgia of 1964 looked like a hotbed of union activity compared with the Georgia of 2006 where plant closings and the threat thereof as well as continuing local resistance in some parts of the state had brought union membership down below 5 percent.

With manufacturing employment in steep decline, Georgia boasted nearly a million more jobs in 2005 than in 1997 only because of the phenomenal expansion of the service economy, which accounted for two-thirds of the state's employment in 2005. Higher-end jobs in healthcare, education, and financial services were clearly an economic boon, but even those who had lost low-wage jobs in the textile and apparel industry often took pay cuts of 30 percent or more working as desk clerks and cashiers or in other such downscale service occupations. The persistence of so much low-wage employment translated into an estimated 584,000 Georgians with at least one fully employed worker in the family who were still eligible for food stamp assistance in 2004. Owing to such a large "working-poor" population in the state at large, by 2000, mobile homes had become an even more prominent feature of the rural landscape, accounting for over half the housing units in four counties and at least a quarter of them in eighty-five.

Though Georgia's political leaders were often quick to criticize Washington for its intrusion into the state's affairs, in light of the dramatic job cutbacks in some industries there was no denying the beneficial impact of federal spending on the state. Georgia's success in attracting major military facilities had paid off especially well. Military installations like Warner Robins's Robins Air Force Base and Columbus's Fort Benning had been absolutely crucial to their local economies for many years. By 2005 Georgia ranked fifth nationally in in-state federal defense spending, which amounted to more than $12.5 billion annually, with full-time military and military-related employment well in excess of combined totals for the state's textile, apparel, and paper industries.

Roughly a million Georgians had lived on farms in 1950, but the steadily shrinking farm population was down to barely sixty thousand in 2002. The ongoing frustration of dealing with the boll weevil, as well as the rise of cotton growing in the Southwest and West, had fueled a continuing post–World War II decline in the state's cotton acreage that culminated in an all-time low of 120,000 acres in 1983. Cotton cultivation began to rebound in Georgia after the launch of a long-awaited boll weevil eradication program at the end of the 1980s, but despite a planting of 1,220,000 acres in 2005, cotton accounted for only 7.5 percent of farm income, barely exceeding the 6 percent attributable to peanuts. In terms of Georgia's overall agricultural economy, however, concealed within the pungent aromas wafting from the state's roughly seven thousand chicken houses was the undeniable odor of money as Georgia led the nation in broiler production, generating $2.4 billion worth in 2005, a figure that represented two and a half times the value of the state's cotton and peanut crops combined. Meanwhile, across the state, much of what had formerly been cropland had been transformed into commercial forests. The forest products industry had become the fourth largest component of the state's economic base by 1980, and as the twenty-first century began, forest products companies controlled over 20 percent of Georgia's forestland and contributed in the neighborhood of $20 billion to the state's economy each year.

Although commercial forests altered Georgia's ecological landscape and local wildlife habitats, they were, on balance, a definite improvement over exhausted, eroded cropland. Nonetheless, the pulp and paper plants that consumed such a large portion of the state's forest products have continued to contribute significantly to its environmental problems. In 2004 more than a dozen pulp and paper manufacturing facilities in Georgia combined to produce some eighteen million pounds of neurotoxicants, such as ammonia and methanol, capable of damaging the central nervous system. Coal-fired power plants were also major producers of neurotoxicants, and ten such Georgia operations added another 4.6 million pounds of these substances to the environment annually. Chief among these facilities was Georgia Power's Plant Bowen, an electric generating plant near Cartersville, which reportedly was the nation's single largest source of the neurotoxicant hydrogen fluoride in 2004. Emissions from Plant Bowen helped to give Cartersville the nation's fourth-heaviest concentration of respiratory toxicants as well. Overall in 2004, Georgia also had the nation's sixth-highest release rate for air- and waterborne carcinogens.

With its extraordinarily congested traffic, metropolitan Atlanta regularly posted some of the nation's highest "smog" levels, and at times, especially in the humid summer months, even smaller metro areas like Macon and Columbus were blanketed by such pollution. A 2007 study showed that a combined fifty-five acres of ground was covered by concrete, asphalt, and roofs every day in Atlanta's growth-mad metropolitan counties, with a corresponding amount of tree cover destroyed daily as well. With experts estimating that the quality of local streams began to deteriorate when as little as 9 percent of their drainage area was paved over, Clayton County, which was home to the massive Hartsfield-Jackson International Airport, showed about 25 percent concrete coverage, with other heavily populated counties like Cobb and Gwinnett approaching 18 percent. Not surprisingly, the water quality of local lakes like Lanier and Allatoona suffered significantly as they were subjected to increasing amounts of grease, dirt, and other runoff pollution.

Pollution was not merely an urban or industrial problem, of course. In addition to the threats posed by pesticides, herbicides, and commercial fertilizers, the more than a million tons of litter generated annually by Georgia's chicken houses contained not only high levels of nitrogen but more phosphorous than the sewage that might normally be generated by 40 million people. Environmentalists warned that when chicken manure is spread on pastures and fields, the nutrient-overrich runoff can stimulate excessive algae growth in streams and lakes, leading ultimately to oxygen deprivation sufficient to kill fish. Some scientists also linked the excess nutrients and algae resulting from poultry litter runoff to the toxic microbe *Pfiesteria piscicida*, which is capable of triggering not just massive fish kills but confusion, memory loss, acute skin irritation, and other forms of distress in humans.

Such environmental concerns may have helped to explain why a long-standing annual ranking of state "health" climates put Georgia in forty-third place in 2005, just one position higher than where it had been fifteen years before. Georgia actually fared better than most other southern states in most traditional health categories, although its forty-first-ranked infant mortality rate, which stood at 23 percent above the national average in 2005, was hardly anything to brag about. This comprehensive analysis also incorporated such nonmedical data as the four-year high school graduation rates for entering ninth graders. Here, at barely 60 percent, Georgia bested only South Carolina, although, interestingly enough, its very close rival for next-to-last place was New York.

Although here again there was little reason to boast, the survey revealed that, following a national trend, Georgians have actually grown less homicidal in recent years. After standing at 22 percent above the national average in 1995, Georgia's murder rate was only 10 percent higher than the national norm in 2005. Like southerners in general, Georgians are more likely to kill or be killed by someone they know. This reality is reflected in the high incidence of men killing women in Georgia. In 2003, 90 percent of the women killed by men in the state had known their killer, the majority as spouses, ex-spouses, and girlfriends. Here it seems, the spread of gang- and drug-related violence, not just into urban and metropolitan areas but out into rural Georgia as well, may have been superimposed over a fading but still sometimes detectable frontier-bred hypermasculinity that demanded female subservience and imposed it by violence if necessary.

THE PAST IS NEVER DEAD

If, whatever the causes, twenty-first-century Georgia remained much too violent a place, it might at least be said that far less of the state's violence was racially motivated than it had been throughout most of the preceding century. In fact, although Georgia clearly still had its problems, its racial climate showed definite signs of improvement. Assuming the data is representative, a comparison of southern opinion surveys from 1988 and 2003 suggests that black Georgians may have become more likely than their northern counterparts to believe racial discrimination was on the wane, while whites may have become significantly more aware that it still existed. One indicator of lowered barriers to black advancement lay in median black household income, which had risen by two-thirds, not just in metro Atlanta but statewide, during the 1990s, a rate of increase 40 percent higher than that for whites. Economic gains for both groups clearly helped to mute some anxieties and resentments, especially at the higher end of the socioeconomic scale. Metro Atlanta's suburbs were among the nation's most racially integrated, and despite evidence of creeping resegregation, the same was true of the state's schools. By 2001 there were more than six hundred black elected officials in Georgia, four of whom were serving in Congress. The changes in Georgia's racial landscape since the civil rights movement were readily apparent in the state legislature, where blacks accounted for 23 percent of the overall membership in 2007 and a majority of the Democratic members of both houses.

Although most black and white leaders recognized that cooperation was clearly preferable to conflict if their state and their communities were to have a better future, the past just kept getting in the way, never more obviously than in the extraordinarily tenacious and exceedingly divisive issue of the state flag. Although it is impossible to know whether the controversy over the flag during the Olympics had actually changed any minds, an October 2000 poll suggested that support among Georgians for retaining the 1956 flag had fallen below 50 percent, with more than three in four African Americans, one in four white Democrats, and almost one in five white Republicans favoring a change.

When the 2001 legislative session opened, facing the threat by black leaders of an economic boycott "100 times worse" than the one engendered by a similar controversy in South Carolina, Governor Roy Barnes moved quickly and quietly to defuse the crisis. Although as a legislator he had voted against observance of the Martin Luther King Jr. holiday in Georgia, after several secret conferences with business, religious, and educational leaders, Barnes proposed a new state flag that carried only a miniaturized version of the previous flag along with four earlier state flags it also commemorated. Barnes warned that continuing divisions over the state flag threatened to "erode four decades of economic progress" and to jeopardize Georgia's position as the South's economic leader. Former legislator Denmark Groover, who had sponsored the legislation that put the Confederate battle flag emblem on the state banner in 1956, backed Barnes by urging his old colleagues to "end this cauldron of discord that adversely affects our lives and the future of our children and grandchildren."

Supporters of the old flag howled that their "heritage" was being highjacked by a group of powerful politicians and business leaders who had capitulated to the "economic terrorism" embodied in a threatened NAACP boycott. Their demands for a statewide referendum on the issue went unheeded, however, and Barnes signed the new flag bill into law only a few hours after its final approval by the state senate on January 31, 2001. Almost immediately, the Georgia governor became the target of constant taunts and harassment by angry "flaggers" demanding a popular vote on restoring the 1956 flag.

In 2002 gubernatorial challenger Sonny Perdue's promise to hold such a referendum helped him to become Georgia's first Republican governor in one hundred thirty years. Perdue's exceptionally strong showing among rural whites upset about the flag doubtless contributed significantly to his election, but his campaign promise began to haunt him almost as soon as the votes were counted. By reopening the flag brouhaha, he had put himself squarely between the powerful business interests whose concerns for the state's image had led them to back Barnes's expeditious flag switch to the hilt and the angry flag partisans who claimed credit for Perdue's election and promised him the same fate as Barnes should he renege on his pledge.

Predictably, Perdue's politically calculated call for a referendum on restoring the controversial 1956 flag in the interest of "healing" the wounds incurred during the long flag battle simply reopened them, triggering numerous bitter, racially tinged public confrontations and legislative votes divided sharply along racial lines. When its political leaders finally realized that the state could stand no more of Perdue's brand of healing, Georgians wound up with yet another state flag, their third in two years, this one based on the original, pre-1956 model derived from the design of the first official flag of the Confederacy. Voters expressed a three to one preference for this latest banner over the Barnes flag in a March 2, 2004, referendum, leading to Democratic state senator George Hooks's foolish announcement that "the flag debate is now a chapter in our history." Sure enough, the very next day a group of fighting-mad flaggers gathered in front of the state capitol to voice their displeasure that, contrary to Perdue's promise, the old massive resistance–era Confederate battle flag design had not even been an option on the ballot. Sounding every bit the unreconstructed rebel, and quite a melodramatic one at that, Kenneth Watters, a spokesman for the group, declared, "We will keep our anger alive. We shall be grim and unconvinced and wear our bitterness like a medal." As for the elected officials who had blocked a vote on the 1956 flag, he warned, "We the flaggers are coming for you."

A GOP STRONGHOLD

Perdue's victory in 2002 was more than a sharp bolt of single-issue anger that quickly receded into the firmament. Georgia had once been nothing less than an impregnable Democratic fortress, but as of 2007, save for Jimmy Carter in 1976 and Bill Clinton in 1992, no Democratic presidential candidate had carried the state since 1960, and none, save Carter, had garnered more than roughly one-third of the white vote. In the early years of the Republican Revolution, local political aspirants often ran as Democrats while sporting bumper stickers and yard signs touting the GOP's presidential candidate, but as Republicanism moved "down the ticket," more and more courthouse offices fell captive to full-fledged, honest-to-goodness Republicans who had brazenly campaigned as such.

By 2002 the Republicans had long been poised for such a takeover in Atlanta, awaiting only a suitable candidate and the right issue. The relative conservatism of their Democratic adversaries and the challenge of organizing campaigns in one hundred fifty-nine counties simultaneously had kept the Republicans in the minority in the Georgia legislature, but they ousted longtime house speaker Tom Murphy and claimed control of the state senate in 2002 before taking control of the house two years later. Both the house and senate had been roughly 80 percent Democratic in 1990, but with the already dwindling Democratic majorities shattered in 2002 and 2004, by 2007 both houses were 60 percent Republican. Georgia's delegation to the House of Representatives reflected this trend, boasting seven Republicans and six Democrats.

Georgia's representation in Washington became decidedly more

Republican in 2002 when Saxby Chambliss ousted incumbent Democratic senator Max Cleland in a campaign that saw Chambliss, with no military service to his credit, challenge the patriotism of his opponent, a legless Vietnam veteran. Two years later, Republican Johnny Isakson joined Chambliss in the Senate. Despite significant Republican losses nationwide in the 2006 congressional elections, in Georgia it was the Democratic incumbents who had trouble holding on to their seats. Some still questioned whether the GOP's triumph was as definitive and irreversible as it seemed, but if the Democrats hoped to reclaim their once lofty perch atop state politics, they would have to find a way to market their more moderate brand of politics to suburban whites who want fiscal responsibility with adequate services but have no interest in confrontations over the state flag and other potentially embarrassing and economically disruptive issues. At the same time, however, with blacks making up the majority of their representation in the legislature and two-thirds of their representation in Congress, Georgia Democrats can ill afford to become so conservative as to alienate the black support that is clearly their party's lifeblood.

NEW OPPORTUNITIES, NEW PRIORITIES

As a group, blacks in Georgia had clearly made enormous strides since the civil rights movement, and by the end of the twentieth century the same might be said of women as well. Although its impact was gradual rather than immediate, Title VII of the Civil Rights Act of 1964 had outlawed employment discrimination by sex as well as by race, and its long-term effect was to open many doors that had long been firmly closed to women. By 1999 the state's working women were paid almost as well as their northern counterparts, and although their earnings still lagged behind those of men, the gap had narrowed more rapidly in Georgia between 1989 and 2005 than in the nation at large.

More than twenty-five years after the ERA was voted down for the final time in the legislature, Georgia stood roughly in the middle of the pack among the states on most issues relating to women. With more than 35 percent of its working women holding down professional and managerial jobs in 2002, the state ranked in the top third in this category. The same was true of the percentage of businesses owned by women (after Georgia moved up ten spots between 1997 and 2002). At the other end of the scale, however, the percentage of women living below the poverty level showed only a negligible decrease between 1995 and 2005, and the state fared equally poorly in other measures related to the health and well-being of women at the lower end of the socioeconomic scale.

On the political front, the Georgia General Assembly included forty-six women in 2007, more than double the number from a decade earlier, and women made up roughly 20 percent of the total legislative membership as compared with 24 percent nationwide. Black women in particular achieved a relatively striking numerical presence in the legislature, claiming nineteen seats and accounting for more than 40 percent of Georgia's female lawmakers. Though they held only 8 percent of all the seats in 2007, that figure was still twice the national average. Meanwhile, Atlanta's Shirley Franklin stood out as one of two black women serving as mayor of one of the nation's one hundred largest cities in 2007.

The situation has also improved for Georgia's school children. The state's commitment to education had grown considerably stronger in the decades after World War II. At the end of the 1920s, Georgia had ranked dead last among the southern states in its support for public education, and twenty years later its standing had improved but little. Over the next thirty years, however, as more political leaders accepted the need to improve schools in the interest of economic development, per-pupil expenditures increased tenfold. By the dawn of the twenty-first century, both these expenditures and teachers' salaries were near the national average. Achievement test scores also approached national norms, although wide disparities in educational achievement levels still separated rural and metropolitan school systems.

In higher education, a generously endowed Emory University moved ahead as one of the nation's most dynamic private institutions, and Georgia Tech won increasing national and international recognition for its engineering programs. The University of Georgia managed to earn a coveted top-twenty slot among public universities in the annual rankings issued by *U.S. News and World Report*, which also made Atlanta's Spelman College the first historically black school to be named America's premier liberal arts college.

Fifteen years after the HOPE Scholarship program's inception in 1993, most observers agreed that the state's colleges and universities have benefited from it substantially. HOPE had made it much more attractive for brighter, more accomplished students to stay in Georgia for their higher education, a factor that was reflected in the steadily rising SAT scores of entering freshmen at the state's institutions. Between 1993 and 2006, Georgia paid over $3.2 billion in HOPE scholarships to more than a million students. The HOPE program had served as a model for similar efforts in some fifteen states, and it remained quite popular with Georgians in general. HOPE had also drawn some critical fire, however. Initial eligibility caps based on family income were removed in 1995, sparking complaints about the state funding a program to subsidize the education of children from affluent homes with a lottery that drew its revenues disproportionately from the lower classes. Researchers found, for example, that parents of HOPE recipients were often inclined to reward their high-achieving offspring with new cars, financed in part with the tuition savings provided by HOPE. Other critics alleged that the program promotes grade inflation at both the high school and the university level. This charge was not without merit, certainly, but the single most surprising — and embarrassing — statistic surrounding HOPE was the retention rate. One study showed that, as of 2004, only 35 percent of HOPE recipients who had entered the state's public institutions as freshmen were still eligible for the scholarship after taking just thirty credit hours of course work (the equivalent of two semesters at full load), and by ninety credit hours the figure was only 29 percent. Some experts insisted that HOPE's retention problem showed that SAT or ACT scores are better predictors of college readiness than are high school grades, but others charged that such tests are inherently biased against black children, who are already disadvantaged by the generally poorer quality of the secondary educations that many of them receive.

NOT JUST BLACK AND WHITE

From the middle of the eighteenth century to the end of the twentieth, politics, law, and many other aspects of life in Georgia could, as often as not, be reduced to fundamental matters of black and white. By the beginning of the twenty-first century, however, questions of race and group identity had, to say the least, become a bit more complicated. Twenty years ago, a reporter could already describe metropolitan Atlanta's multiethnic Buford Highway as "Chinatown, Little Moscow, and the Latin Quarter melded into one" and perhaps the only place in the Southeast "where you can listen to a sermon in Korean, get tax advice in Vietnamese, and rent a Cantonese or Spanish video." In Chamblee and Doraville, the Asian population had more than doubled during the 1980s, while the Hispanic population more than quadrupled. Even farther out, in the Gainesville area, the number of Hispanic residents swelled by more than 725 percent during the same decade, accounting for more than 20 percent of Hall County's population increase over that period.

These trends were but harbingers of things to come as Georgia's Hispanic population increased by 300 percent in the 1990s. Although Hispanics still accounted for only 19 percent of the state's overall population growth, in smaller towns especially, the new Hispanic presence was difficult to miss. Bisected by the now even more intensely multicultural Buford Highway, Doraville saw its Hispanic population explode from 9 percent in 1990 to 54 percent in 2007. (Doraville's Asian residents accounted for an additional 13 percent, meaning that the two groups accounted for two-thirds of the local population by 2007.) Despite a population of only ten thousand, Doraville had nonetheless become Georgia's most strikingly internationalized community. Eyebrows were definitely raised, however, when towns less than half its size began sporting both multiple Mexican restaurants (where proprietors and many diners actually spoke Spanish) and Mexican specialty markets (along with greatly expanded Mexican food sections in the local Ingles or Bi-Lo). Likewise, it hardly escaped notice down in South Georgia when students at Atkinson County High, whose student body had changed from 4 percent Hispanic in 1994 to 26 percent Hispanic in 2006, elected a Hispanic couple as homecoming king and queen.

Since the average twenty-first-century Hispanic newcomer had neither a high school diploma nor much of an acquaintance with English, small, already underequipped and understaffed rural school systems faced a major challenge in trying to teach children who had been raised by undereducated parents in homes where the only English they heard came from the television. Men outnumbered women among Hispanic immigrants, but typically twenty-something newlywed couples were extremely prolific, and the birth rate among Hispanics easily surpassed that of blacks as well as whites, suggesting that the stresses on the school systems would only become more pronounced.

There was no shortage of complaints that Hispanics were taking jobs away from other Georgians, but in general, Hispanic employment grew fastest in precisely the same areas where whites and blacks were also finding more opportunities. The number of Hispanic workers increased by well over 500 percent in Cherokee County in the 1990s, but over the decade, non-Hispanics claimed seven times more jobs than Hispanics. Among counties with the fastest growing Hispanic populations, only in Whitfield, where a concentration of carpet mills drew Hispanic workers in large numbers, did non-Hispanic employment actually decline. In view of all the political furor over immigration restriction, a surprisingly small percentage of those polled, roughly one in four as of 2002, believed that immigrants were taking jobs that would otherwise have gone to native Georgians.

This view was not necessarily representative of all black Georgians, however, particularly those who saw themselves in direct competition for jobs with Hispanic immigrants, who were often willing to work dirt cheap, sometimes under grossly substandard conditions. The jobless rate for black men in Georgia was nearly three times that for Hispanic men in 2006. In Atkinson County, the black county clerk, Joyce Taylor, predicted that if there were any new factory openings thereabouts, "Hispanics would get the majority of the jobs."

A 2006 report indicating that Georgia had the nation's fastest-growing illegal immigrant population spurred angry calls for tighter enforcement of immigration laws. Efforts to crack down on illegals, however, frequently demonstrated how vital they had become to certain sectors of the state's economy. After a 2006 Labor Day–weekend raid by federal immigration officials cost them roughly 75 percent of the work force at their Stillmore, Georgia, chicken processing plant, Crider, Inc., executives boosted pay rates by more than a dollar an hour and hired about two hundred new workers from the Southeast Georgia region, most of them black. This seemed to suggest that Hispanics had, in fact, been claiming jobs that would have gone to locals, but it was not long before disputes over wages and working conditions began to surface. Plant managers complained of declining productivity and rising absenteeism, which the remaining Hispanics in the workforce blamed on their new black coworkers.

By January 2007 Crider had begun to recruit new employees among Laotian Hmong immigrants living in Minnesota. A few months later, still operating with fewer than half the workers they had employed prior to the raid, desperate Crider executives struck a deal with the Georgia Department of Corrections to bus in some forty probationers who could use their wages to pay off fines and defray the cost of housing them at a state diversion center. Crider's difficulties only underscored the willingness of Hispanic immigrants to work at wages and under conditions that few Americans would accept. For blacks trying to improve their economic standing, the implications of the Hispanic influx were clear and menacing. The resulting tensions between Hispanics and blacks could turn violent, as seemed to be the case when four black men were arrested for the robbery and murder of six Mexican farm workers near Tifton in November 2006.

In the political arena, despite talk on both sides of the need for black-Hispanic unity in the struggle against poverty and discrimination, some black lawmakers fought a 2001 bill that would have made Hispanic businesses eligible for a state program designed to assist minority enterprises. Although Hispanics now had at least a measure of legislative representation themselves, compared with their black counterparts, their representatives hardly spoke in one voice. Of the four Hispanics who had been elected to the state legislature by 2007, the two Democrats, state senator Sam Zamarrippa of Atlanta and Representative Pedro Marin of Duluth, had supported granting driver's licenses to illegal immigrants and making HOPE scholarships available to their children while opposing efforts to crack down on illegals and those who employ them. On the other hand, their Republican colleagues, Representatives David Casas of Lilburn and Tony Sellier of Fort Valley, had argued against any concessions to illegals and supported legislation to restrict their access to government services. Casas had also worried that too many Hispanics in Georgia "are still tied to their native country. . . . If you come to the United States, you have to be able to say, 'This is my country now.'"

METROPOLITAN CONSERVATIVES

The widening economic gap between the residents of metropolitan Atlanta and those living in Georgia's rural areas had manifested itself in differences in lifestyles and tastes, but the political distance between the two groups proved narrower on some issues than most had expected.

For years, observers had predicted that in combination with an influx of in-migrants from outside the region, the urbanization of the South's population would undermine the conservative values that seemed so deeply rooted in rural and small-town areas. In Georgia, as elsewhere, this prediction sometimes went more than slightly awry. As its residents left the countryside in search of greater opportunity, instead of urbanizing according to the classic pattern, Georgia "metropolitanized" or "suburbanized," owing primarily to the fact that its economic transformation came well after the advent of the automobile, allowing workers to live at some distance from their jobs instead of clustering in cities to be near them. Georgia's extensive network of interstate highways (Atlanta is one of only five cities nationwide where three interstate highways intersect) ultimately facilitated this process. By 1990 nearly two-thirds of all Georgians lived in metropolitan areas; a decade later the portion was three-fourths.

Although they were markedly less concerned with symbolic issues like retaining the Confederate battle emblem as part of the state flag, on other matters that affected them more directly, whites in metropolitan Atlanta sometimes proved only marginally less conservative than their cousins in the countryside. In the 1970s many whites in the adjoining counties were at pains to conceal their racial anxieties when they raised vociferous opposition to extending the Metropolitan Atlanta Rapid Transit Authority's (MARTA) train service into their communities. Despite the prospect of more convenient access to downtown, they were concerned that MARTA, disdainfully redubbed by some to signify "Moving Africans Rapidly Through Atlanta," might make their own secure bedroom communities too readily accessible to the central city's lower-class black population.

Atlanta's affluent suburban counties found themselves at odds with the culturally diverse central city on other volatile social concerns. The growth and increasing activism of Atlanta's gay and lesbian community sparked controversy on a variety of fronts. Over its twenty-five-year history the annual Hotlanta River Expo became the centerpiece for one of the largest gay gatherings in the nation and exemplified the increasing openness of the gay lifestyle in and around the city. Ironically, the event, featuring a giant raft race, was staged on and about the Chattahoochee River, which served as a sort of moat between Atlanta and ultraconservative Cobb County to the north.

Fed by in-migration and white flight from Atlanta, Cobb's 88 percent white population grew from less than two hundred thousand in 1970 to more than five hundred thousand by 1990. Approximately one-third of its residents were college graduates in 1990, as compared with less than one-tenth in 1970, and median household income was more than 30 percent higher than the national average. Cobb County had been the site of the infamous Leo Frank lynching in 1915, and it was represented in Congress by former John Birch Society activist Larry McDonald until his death in 1982. The city council of the Cobb County town of Kennesaw made headlines worldwide when it enacted an ordinance in 1982 requiring each head of household to own not just a gun but also the ammunition for it.

Gay culture came under direct assault in Cobb County in the summer of 1993 as Marietta's Theatre in the Square offered a production of *Lips Together, Teeth Apart*, a play that contained references to AIDS and gay neighbors. Controversy over this production culminated in a county commission resolution declaring that the gay lifestyle was "incompatible with the standards to which this community subscribes" and purporting to send a "message to policy makers of this country such that a previously silent voice will now be heard." As the commission debated, supporters and opponents of the resolution massed outside, with one of the supporters carrying a sign reading "Praise God for AIDS." Commissioners also voted to withhold all public funding for the arts lest some of the funds be spent to promote the homosexual lifestyle.

Gay activists launched a spiritual counteroffensive, staging a "Queer

Family Picnic" in Marietta and spearheading an effort to divert businesses from Cobb County, which had just constructed a forty-three-million-dollar convention center. As did the controversy over the state flag, the Cobb County brouhaha soon spilled over into preparations for the 1996 Olympic Games. Atlanta gay rights groups protested vigorously the Olympic Committee's decision to hold the Olympic volleyball competition in Cobb County. "Olympics Out of Cobb" was the theme at the 1994 Lesbian and Gay Pride Festival, which attracted well over a hundred thousand participants. Although the county commission's action enjoyed considerable support outside Interstate 285 (Atlanta's equivalent to Washington's beltway), the threat of continued protests and the calls of various organizations for gays and lesbians to flock to Atlanta in 1996 ultimately led Olympic organizing officials to withdraw the volleyball competition from Cobb County.

Over the next decade, Atlanta's reputation as one of the nation's most gay-friendly cities continued to build as tourism gurus touted it as "the ideal gay travel destination" because of its ever-expanding variety of clubs, restaurants, and special events aimed at attracting a gay clientele. In 2006 an estimated three hundred thousand people attended Pride Atlanta, an annual gay pride festival that began in 1970 and now generated at least twenty million dollars for the local economy each year.

Cobb County, meanwhile, maintained its growth momentum quite nicely, gaining more than one hundred thousand residents through net migration between 1990 and 2005 while seeing its nonwhite population rise from 12 to 28 percent. The county's fiercely conservative profile has also remained intact, thanks to a dispute over teaching evolution in the public schools that culminated in a school board decree (ultimately voided by the courts) that certain textbooks should bear the following label: "This textbook contains material on evolution. Evolution is a theory, not a fact, regarding the origin of living things. This material should be approached with an open mind, studied carefully, and critically considered."

Cobb County's militant stand on issues such as gay rights and the teaching of evolution had frequently been attributed to the state's conservative religious, particularly Southern Baptist, heritage. Yet scarcely one-third of Cobb's residents in 2000 were even native Georgians, and the Southern Baptist presence in the county fell well short of the state average. For that matter, only 46 percent of its population described themselves as religious adherents of any sort, compared with 58 percent in supposedly wicked Fulton County. Like so many aspects of life in Georgia, its religious milieu presented an intriguing amalgam of continuity and change. Although the state remained securely fixed within the proverbial Bible Belt, the economic and demographic forces that had left nothing untouched had also revealed themselves in the way Georgians worshipped and believed. In 1990, 58 percent of Georgia's population belonged to some religious denomination. By 2000 that percentage had dropped to 45, although in counties like Appling, the proportion of religious adherents was still nearly 80 percent. In all likelihood, to meet a Georgia churchgoer was still to meet a Baptist, but while there were roughly a million more Baptists in Georgia in 2000 than there were in 1950, they now represented 25 rather than 35 percent of the total population. By way of contrast, Roman Catholics, who accounted for less than 6 percent of the religious adherents in Georgia in 1990, represented roughly 10 percent of them a decade later, with much but certainly not all of that growth concentrated in the Atlanta metropolitan area. These shifts notwithstanding, the dominant religious subgroup in Georgia remained the Southern Baptists, whose intense focus on individual salvation had traditionally meant a stronger emphasis on evangelical than social welfare concerns. Forty-seven percent of Georgia's church members were Southern Baptists in 2000, but this group was hardly monolithic. Philosophical and doctrinal differences between moderates and fundamentalists abounded and often erupted into open conflict, especially in larger rural and small-town churches where community demographics were in flux.

Meanwhile, in keeping with the "bigger is better and wealthier is better still" philosophy that appeared to hold sway in other fast-growing southern states like Texas and Florida, Georgia ranked fourth in the nation in 2000 as a home for two-thousand-member-plus mega-churches. Some fifteen thousand adults attended services each week at one of Northpoint Ministries' three locations in the Atlanta area, but the highest-profile and most controversial megachurch in the state was the Atlanta-based and predominantly black, twenty-five-thousand-member World Changers International Church, pastored by the inimitable and aptly named Rev. Creflo Dollar. As the minister of what, with a reported annual budget in excess of $80 million, was reputedly America's "wealthiest megachurch," Dollar preached the "prosperity gospel" that explained "Why God Wants You Rich," and as the owner of two Rolls Royces who also scooted across the country in a Gulfstream jet, he clearly practiced what he preached.

Dollar's focus on the material as well as the spiritual was not unlike that of his fellow megachurch minister Bishop Eddie Long, whose New Birth Missionary Baptist Church likewise claimed twenty-five thousand members and sported a ten-thousand-seat auditorium. Long drew criticism for reportedly receiving some three million dollars and various perks including the use of a $350,000 Bentley from a charity he had organized. Many black ministers had once played key roles in the civil rights movement and other organizing efforts. Now, with Atlanta's upwardly mobile black middle-class population swelling by the day, some congregations seemed more interested in making the most of their own opportunities than in spreading those opportunities around, and both Dollar and Long were professed social and political conservatives who endorsed Republican rather than Democratic candidates and political positions.

Long sparked controversy by leading a 2004 march against same-sex marriage that began at the King Center. The march was all the more noteworthy because Long was accompanied by one of his associate pastors, Rev. Bernice King, the daughter of the great crusader for civil rights. Controversy also erupted when Coretta Scott King died in 2006 and her children chose to hold her funeral in the spacious and swanky New Birth Church in Lithonia instead of the smaller but symbolically powerful Ebenezer Baptist Church, which had been the base of her husband's civil rights and spiritual ministries.

THE BUBBA BOURGEOISIE

Although many expected that the "bulldozer revolution" accompanying urbanization and industrialization would scrape away the last vestiges of southernness, sociologist John Shelton Reed has found, paradoxically enough, that those white southerners most positively affected by the economic and demographic changes that transformed the South seem to be those most interested in clinging to their identity as southerners. In Reed's words, "It is those who are most modern in background and experience . . . who . . . are most likely to think in regional terms, to categorize themselves and others as 'Southerners' and 'non-Southerners' and to believe they know what that means." As if to underscore Reed's argument, across the state each month thousands of upwardly mobile Georgians dote on the latest issue of *Southern Living* in much the same fashion as their less-affluent ancestors once pored dreamily over the pages of the Sears Roebuck catalog.

The identity concerns of many of these comfortably fixed, self-assertive contemporary southerners shaped what Hardy Jackson has called the "bourgeois Bubba" humor of Lewis Grizzard. Conservative — and sometimes downright intolerant and reactionary — Grizzard epitomized the ambivalence of many white southerners who have embraced the economic and material benefits that have come their way while remaining skeptical and sometimes resentful of some of the social and political changes that have accompanied these gains.

Grizzard became sports editor of the *Athens Daily News* at nineteen and held the same position at the *Atlanta Journal* by the time he was twenty-one. After leaving the *Journal* in 1975 for a brief stint as a freelance writer, he journeyed north to join the sports staff of the *Chicago Sun-Times*, where he became executive sports editor. Miserably homesick and freezing, Grizzard literally begged for the chance to leave Chicago in April 1977 and took a twelve-thousand-dollar pay cut to become a sports columnist for the *Atlanta Constitution*. He detailed his experiences as a newspaperman and his odyssey in the frozen North in *If I Ever Get Back to Georgia, I'm Gonna Nail My Feet to the Ground*.

Grizzard had never worked as a columnist, but his return to Atlanta marked the beginning of a remarkable rise to fame. Leaving the sports pages behind, he went on to see his column of southern-style social commentary syndicated in 450 newspapers and to write 20 books, many based on themes and stories he had introduced in his columns. Grizzard also became a popular entertainer, commanding as much as twenty thousand dollars per performance and recording a number of comedy albums. His small-town boyhood and adolescence in tiny Moreland, Georgia, provided him with a huge repertoire of stories about local characters (usually caricatures thereof). A master storyteller, he laced his stories with country colloquialisms such as "he was bad to drink" or "come up a real bad cloud." (The former is self-explanatory; the latter describes the onset of a severe thunderstorm.) His candid country-boy perspective shaped his reaction to all his experiences. In a hilarious story titled "There Ain't No Toilet Paper in Russia," he described Peter the Great's palace as "fifteen times bigger than Opryland."

An unabashed participant in rat killings and other such rustic amusements as a youth, the well-traveled Grizzard nonetheless confessed to having twice seen Pavoratti live (once in Paris and once in London), to having sat through at least the first act of *The Marriage of Figaro*, and to having visited the Louvre. To compound matters, Grizzard owned two pairs of Gucci loafers, wore Geoffrey Beene cologne, and used the gun rack behind the seat of his truck to hold his golf clubs.

Yet, although he had eaten caviar at Maxim's in Paris, Grizzard insisted that he liked pork barbecue better. He reveled in his "redneck" heritage and did not hesitate to remind "transplanted Yankees" who deliver "long diatribes about the South's shortcomings" that "Delta is ready when you are." Plagued by a congenital heart problem and reluctant to curb his rambunctious lifestyle, Grizzard narrowly escaped death during heart surgery in 1993, and hence his last book proclaimed *I Took a Lickin' and Kept On Tickin' and Now I Believe in Miracles*. Grizzard survived to see his beloved Georgia Bulldogs through one more season and to mourn the passing of his faithful dog Catfish. He ran out of miracles, however, in March 1994 when complications from high-risk heart surgery caused the brain damage that took his life at age forty-seven. Grizzard's last days were as poignant as his stories were funny. Only a few hours before his final surgery, he married (in the hospital) for the fourth time. His death was mourned by readers and fans around the nation, but nowhere as intensely in the South and especially in Georgia.

WHO'S A GEORGIAN?

No element of Lewis Grizzard's persona endeared him more to his readership than his ill-concealed distaste for the Yankees who suddenly seemed to be not only overrunning Georgia again but actually planning to stick around this time. Tensions along these lines gradually began to ease a bit as locals grew more accustomed to having these newcomers around, and the newcomers finally realized that the way things were done back in Ohio was a matter of little interest to their new neighbors. Still, as we have seen, sensitivity to criticism has long been common among Georgians, and understandably so, given their state's turbulent past and controversial reputation. Beginning as the noblest of social experiments, Georgia quickly became a haven for profiteering and human exploitation. Though it produced some of the antebellum era's wealthiest and most influential figures, it got (and still gets) a bum rap as a dumping ground for the down and out and, worse yet, the criminal as well. For much of Georgia's history, the dubious designation as "Crackers" stuck to its people like the state's famous red clay. During the secession crisis, Georgia's decision seemed absolutely crucial to the success of the southern independence effort, but after suffering both the torching of Atlanta and Sherman's March to the Sea, the state could not escape widespread popular association with an entire region's defeat and degradation. Even Henry Grady's ballyhoo about Atlanta's rise from the ashes did little to undermine Georgia's reputation as a pathetic symbol of a beaten-down and backward South.

When the nation plunged into World War II, raw statistical comparisons may have indicated that two or three of its southern neighbors were in sadder shape, but as a land rife with racial violence, the site of the Leo Frank lynching, the birthplace of the modern Ku Klux Klan, and a state grown infamous for the brutality of its penal system and the depravity of its demagogues, Georgia boasted stellar credentials to represent the southern way of life at its worst.

In *The Mind of the South*, W. J. Cash had argued that the South of 1940 still bore a strong resemblance to the South of 1840 and stressed resistance to change as the key to the survival of a distinctive southern identity. Certainly, there were few Georgians in 1940 who would have predicted the dramatic changes that would soon be sweeping across their state. Yet historian George B. Tindall has observed that "to change is not necessarily to lose one's identity; to change sometimes is to find it." Georgia's recent experience underscores Tindall's point, for it suggests not an end but a beginning as Georgians embarked on a voyage of self-discovery, one that, hopefully, would lead to widespread rejection of what Katharine Du Pre Lumpkin called "the old dogma, that but one way was Southern, and hence there could be but one kind of Southerner."

Georgia has clearly come a long way since Eugene Talmadge dismissed as a "furriner" anyone "who attempts to impose ideas that are counter to the established traditions of Georgia." However, this is not to say that Talmadge's point of view died quickly or without a struggle.

Witness the Savannah lawyer who argued in January 1993 that "when a true Georgian looks at the [state] flag with its Confederate emblem, he sees the beauty of his Southern heritage." As *Atlanta Journal-Constitution* columnist Colin Campbell pointed out, at the time, to deny the designation "Georgian" to anyone who refused to embrace the "Confederatized" state flag was effectively to exclude (in all likelihood) most of the nearly two million blacks, many of them natives, who lived in the state, as well as a sizable number of other residents born and raised elsewhere in the nation and the world.

Anyone who failed to see Campbell's latter point needed only to head out from Atlanta up Buford Highway, of course. Although it apparently still hadn't registered with folks who, even as the twenty-first century unfolded, continued to yell "Carpetbagger" at anyone who dared suggest the state could benefit from a few changes, it had long been utterly impossible to identify either a "true Georgian" or, in Eugene Talmadge's words, "the established traditions of Georgia" to which "true Georgians" are bound to adhere.

Yet despite our inability to reduce ourselves and our values to a handy composite profile, the majority of us continue to see ourselves as southerners in general and Georgians in particular even if we might not agree about what that means. Here again, the state flag controversy made this abundantly clear. John Head, who grew up in Jackson, rejected the suggestions of a pro-flag partisan that "black people aren't really Southerners," and insisted, "The South is my home.... I am a Southerner." Head simply refused, he explained, "to allow others to say what that means," just as he declined to "accept the Confederacy as the South at its best" or to "accept the Confederate battle flag as an emblem in which all Georgians can take pride." Head went on, "I criticize the South, not just because I believe it does not do well enough, but because I know it can do better. Love, not hate, is the basis for that criticism."

Black Georgians had been raising critical concerns for generations, but as Head's comments suggested, in the aftermath of the civil rights movement, they spoke not as disaffected exiles in their own land but as bona fide insiders who felt a genuine sense of involvement in the affairs of state and society. As the 1996 Olympics drew near, novelist Tina McElroy Ansa proclaimed herself "a child of Atlanta" and "a daughter of Georgia," who wanted Atlanta "to look as spiffy to the world as any staunch city booster."

Ansa was particularly proud of "Atlanta's well-earned image as a beacon of conscience . . . a place that forged the conscience of Martin Luther King Jr. and W. E. B. Du Bois and *Constitution* editor Ralph McGill," and she worried that Olympic-inspired efforts to accentuate Atlanta's positives might lead to neglect of the plight of the city's poor and homeless, a number of whom might be displaced as a result of the games. Ansa believed the key to showing the world that Atlanta's moral conviction was genuine and strong lay in "how we treat the weak as well as the strong, the down-at-the-heel as well as the well-heeled, the slow as well as the swift." To Ansa, once the games were over and the crowds had gone home, the big question would be "How will we Georgians, we Atlantans feel about the Olympic image we presented to the world and, more importantly, to ourselves?"

Although her enrollment as one of the first two black students at the University of Georgia had sparked a riot in 1961, when Charlayne Hunter-Gault returned to her alma mater as a commencement speaker, her message to a still overwhelmingly white graduating class was neither defiant nor bitter. Instead, she offered her own surprisingly positive assessment of a contemporary southern identity reshaped by change but retaining a vital and almost inspiring distinctiveness. "As we shared our destiny," Hunter-Gault observed, "I believe we came to know each other in new aspects, and I believe we came to acknowledge and respect both each other's abilities and each other's ways of life." She described the South as the nation's only "true melting pot," explaining that "through the events of our toil and our tumultuous history we have become a definable people."

Born under Jim Crow in Memphis and living in Atlanta after a brief sojourn in the North, Larry Conley agreed that "this connection to the past—even a past that was often brutal and ugly and stupid—in a strange way binds Southerners together. It's our past, good and bad, and we take equal ownership of it." Conley was but one of many African American southerners who made the decision to return and stake their claims on their homeland. Led by Atlanta, Georgia posted the nation's highest net gains in black population by in-migration between 1975 and 2000. Like Conley and many other returnees, after living in eight states, Savannah native Harold Jackson concluded, "I'd rather be in the South than any place else." Part of Georgia's attraction was certainly its economic dynamism, but, as Jackson put it, "It's not just that the opportunities are here. It's that the opportunities to solve the problems that exist are here, too."

Orion Douglass felt much the same. After growing up in segregated Savannah and spending time in the Northeast and Midwest, Douglass returned to Brunswick, where he won a judgeship in a county that was nearly 80 percent white. Douglas received his legal training in the North, but after getting a taste of northern urban life, he saw Georgia as a place where "I had a better chance of being who I could be. . . . I think I've done better here than I could have done anyplace else."

Though by no means all black Georgians were as upbeat as Jackson and Douglass, many seemed to take heart in knowing that they lived in a state where, when all the pluses and minuses had been tallied, things had changed decidedly for the better in recent years. For all the tangible evidence of progress, however, this sense of identification with Georgia and the South was rooted not only in empirical reality but in an almost spiritual longing for kinship with both people and place, the kind of attachments forged and articulated not only by writers like Alice Walker, Tina McElroy Ansa, and Raymond Andrews but by a great many others less inclined to express their feelings so openly. Many years ago, Richard Weaver had insisted that "being a southerner is definitely a spiritual condition, like being a Catholic or a Jew, and members of the group can recognize one another by signs which are eloquent to them, though too small to be noticed by an outsider." At the time of Weaver's observation, "southerner" was a designation reserved for whites only, but although they were not always terribly specific, many more contemporary South watchers insisted that, regardless of race, as they interacted with each other, southerners could draw on a certain common sensibility and intuition. As John Shelton Reed explained, "Shared understandings . . . make communication easier, and these are the kinds of things people tend to mention these days when you ask them what makes the South what it is."

Georgia writer Mary Hood offered a hypothetical illustration of Reed's point that is likely to resonate with anyone who has asked a long-time rural Georgian to identify someone:

> Suppose a man is walking across a field. To the question "Who is that?" a Southerner would reply by saying something like "Wasn't his granddaddy the one whose dog and him got struck by lightning on the steel bridge? Mama's third cousin — dead before my time — found his railroad watch in that eight-pound catfish's stomach the next summer just above the dam. I think it was eight pounds. Big as Eunice's arm. The way he married for that new blue Cadillac automobile, reckon how come he's walking like he has on Sunday shoes, if that's who it is, and for sure it is." A Northerner would reply to the same question (only if directly asked, though, never volunteering), "That's Joe Smith." To which the Southerner might think (but be much too polite to say aloud), "They didn't ask his name, they asked who he *is*!"

Finding such impressionistic evidence a rather flimsy premise on which to stake a claim to cultural distinctiveness, a number of external critics and even a few southerners themselves worried that the zealous insistence on the continuing significance of southernness had degenerated into an exercise in mythologizing and self-caricature. Certainly the outlines and features of the contemporary southern (and Georgian) identity were subjective and inconsistent at best, especially compared with the strikingly clear and starkly recognizable portrait drawn by W. J. Cash over fifty years ago. However, Cash's sharper imagery resulted in large part from his narrower focus — on the mind of the white male South, a mind clearly circumscribed by racial anxieties, gender constraints, and sectional antagonism. A socially and economically transformed and demographically diversified Georgia, where the opinions of minorities and women mattered more and the question of race less, presented a warmer but also fuzzier and, in some ways, no less contradictory picture. Along these lines, not too long ago, an *Atlanta Journal-Constitution* poll (including both black and white respondents) showed southerners listing both country music and the blues and both Robert E. Lee and Martin Luther King Jr. as relevant symbols of their South. Needless to say, the recent Hispanic influx has made the definition of regional and state identity subject to even greater change.

This situation was hardly a new one. Over the course of their state's history, Georgians have constantly revised and reshaped their identity, often embracing the symbols of both tradition and change as their own. For example, "I'm just an old Georgia Cracker" soon became a disarmingly self-deprecatory reference, and for years, the minor league Atlanta Crackers were more than a minor passion for the state's baseball fans.

Tourists and newcomers to Georgia often expressed both amusement and dismay at some of the state's dietary mainstays, especially grits. Rather than apologize for this local delicacy, Roy Blount Jr. took the offensive, paying tribute to:

> True grits, more grits, fish, grits and collards,
> Life is good where grits are swallered.

On the other side of the ledger, despite their reputation for conservatism, Georgians were quick to incorporate into their culture any number of the changes that came their way under the general heading of "progress." The tenacious popularity of moonshine in some quarters notwithstanding, Coca-Cola quickly achieved widespread acceptance as the state's beverage of choice, so much so that even when a thirsty Georgian intended to drink a Pepsi, he or she was nonetheless likely to say, "Let's go get a 'Co-Coler.'"

Although tourists often joked about the prodigious patches of kudzu that blanketed roadsides and seemed to swallow utility poles, abandoned automobiles, and vacant houses overnight, the fast-growing plant, originally imported from Japan to combat soil erosion, quickly took root as the state's unofficial vine. From one end of Georgia to the other, communities with no better premise for celebration or self-promotion sponsored annual kudzu festivals replete with bake sales and beauty pageants culminating in the selection of a kudzu queen. James Dickey even saw fit to immortalize these fast-growing "Far Eastern Vines" in verse, noting that

> In Georgia, the legend says
> That you must close your windows
> At night to keep it out of the house.

First-time sojourners through the kudzu-clad Georgia countryside might relate as well to these slightly altered musings of would-be poet Frank Gannon:

> What this is
> I do not know
> There is a hell of a lot of it [though].

Unreconstructed Georgians might have taken a certain smug satisfaction in reports that, owing to global warming, kudzu was rapidly moving north. At the same time, however, wistful observers noted that, despite an occasional patch here and there, the pesky "state vine" was rapidly receding toward the endangered-species list in Atlanta, offering what some might have seen as an apt metaphor for that city's dwindling association with Georgia and the South in general. A 1996 poll revealed that fewer than half the southerners or nonsoutherners contacted believed Atlanta remained a "distinctively southern" city. Likewise, even before the Olympics, when pollsters asked "what the city of Atlanta is noted for, nationally and internationally," the most common responses dealt with associations (good and bad) that had been formed relatively recently:

RESPONSE	% OF ALL RESPONSES
Olympics	28.8
The Braves	10.8
Crime	7.9
Business/Industry/Jobs	5.8

Compare these with the percentage of respondents choosing more "traditional" regional associations with Atlanta:

RESPONSE	% OF ALL RESPONSES
Hospitality	3.0
Gone with the Wind	2.2
Southern/South	1.3

Since these surveys were taken, suffice it to say, incidents such as the dismissal in 2002 of Moby, a local country music disk jockey whose accent was deemed too "country" for his Atlanta audience, have done little to resouthernize the city's image.

NOUVELLE GEORGIA: TRADITIONAL MEETS TRENDY

In reality, rather than choose between old and new, like their fellow Georgians in general, Atlantans have often opted to blend or simply juxtapose the two, much like an electronic message board at the city's Peachtree Baptist Church that read, "Being Born Again Means Being Plugged Into A New Power Source." Despite their cosmopolitan pretensions, Atlanta's ever-entrepreneurial boosters were clearly not above catering to stereotypically southern cultural tastes if there was money on the table. Development leaders opted in 2006 to make a last-minute and somewhat quixotic bid to make Atlanta the home of the future

NASCAR Museum and Hall of Fame. Touting its projected economic impact, proponents argued the NASCAR shrine could be located near the Georgia Aquarium, allowing the two attractions to draw on each other's clientele. Had this come to pass, one observer joked, the aquarium folks might have been forced to put in a quick order for some No Fishing signs, but such a move proved unnecessary when the NASCAR execs had the temerity to choose Atlanta's upstart rival Charlotte, North Carolina, as the home of the museum.

The peaceful coexistence of old and new sometimes came through in Atlantans' dining preferences as well. In the mid-1980s, as I attempted to unravel the "enigma of Sunbelt Georgia," I noted the simultaneous popularity of "cracklin's and caviar" in a culturally ambivalent Atlanta where diners scrambled with equal fervor for tables at the ultrachic Nikolai's Roof (atop the Hilton downtown) and the decidedly down-home Harold's Barbecue (near the federal penitentiary on McDonough Boulevard). More than two decades later, Nikolai's Roof had clearly lost some of its exotic appeal (though only because of a slew of worthy high-end competitors like Bacchanalia and the Dining Room at the Ritz-Carlton, Buckhead), but recent visitors to Harold's reported no such loss of allure. Indeed, the waitresses still called diners "honey" and "sugah," and the cracklin' corn bread remained — pun intended — a heavy favorite on the menu. Meanwhile, Southeast met Far East in the deep-fried collard green rolls with sweet chili sauce at Cenci and Middle East in the butterbean hummus at Watershed. Beyond Atlanta, in a number of smaller cities and even towns, popular restaurants featured "nouvelle southern" cuisine blending the exotic with the familiar. Diners at Five and Ten in Athens might well find themselves choosing among halibut with saffron broth, grilled chicken with squash casserole, and the house specialty, Frogmore Stew, and many a high-end entrée has come to the table accompanied by Red Mule grits.

Changes in foodways have also mirrored the larger changes in rural and small-town life. At last count, forty-six cents of every dining-out dollar spent in Georgia goes for fast food. (This may help to explain why Georgia ranked as the nation's twelfth-most obese state in 2007.) In my little town of Hartwell, "progress" could certainly be measured in terms of the appearance of fast-food chain restaurants. The Dairy Queen arrived in the 1950s, followed at some length by a Tastee-Freez. Much later came a Hardee's (which at least fixed decent biscuits), a Pizza Hut, and a Kentucky Fried Chicken. Hartwell's true emergence as a place to be reckoned with, however, came only when the fabled Golden Arches of McDonald's became a part of its skyline. Hardee's eventually became a casualty of the battle of the burger joints; even in Georgia, man does not live by biscuit alone, it seems. Not intimidated in the least, however, Arby's showed up soon thereafter, situating itself defiantly across the street from the Golden Arches. Burger King came a bit later, as did Wendy's and Sonic, and finally Zaxby's Chicken.

On the higher end of the food chain, first came Vickery Parke, which advertised and delivered genuine fine dining with the meals prepared by a skilled, professionally trained chef. Not long ago, however, Vickery Parke succumbed to the somewhat broader though still decidedly up-scale appeal of the Waterfall Grille at the Cateechee Golf Club, which also offers liquor by the drink through some legal loophole that local Baptists could not manage to plug. The popularity of Cateechee's restaurant said something about the changes in palates and pocketbooks in the area, but just on the other side of town, the Swamp Guinea was still swamped with diners feasting on deep-fried catfish, shrimp, and chicken.

Even the outlying rural areas of Hart County were caught up from time to time in this uneven process of foodways in transition. A decade or so ago, I drove for the first time in many years through the Reed Creek community whence my mama's people came and observed in what had been the remotest and "roughest" part of the county a new restaurant called the Reed Creek Trattoria. This pleasant little establishment shared a crossroads with a gas station and a hardware store, and on its front door a sign offered the following definition: "Trattoria — A place to eat; restaurant, casual, informal cafe. Fresh, simple food found throughout Italy and Reed Creek!" Inexorable as they might be, however, the forces of change retreat as well as advance. On a subsequent visit to Reed Creek, I discovered that Reed Creek Trattoria had given way to Me-Maw's, which offered diners no definitions but the traditional "meat and two" (vegetables) plus bread and dessert for $3.99 (beverage not included).

Me-Maw's flourished for a while, especially during deer season when hungry hunters sought out the hearty but somewhat heavy fare, but before long the familiar once again gave way to the exotic in the form of Gumbo Charlie's Crabhouse. Cajun cuisine seemed a bit hard on the tummy to some local folks, but Gumbo Charlie's offered the undeniably novel and entertaining spectacle of the first live-lobster tank anybody could remember sighting in Reed Creek. In the long run, however, she-crab soup and shrimp étouffée proved fairly thin gruel for some diners, a good many of whom spent their workdays on tractors and backhoes, and Gumbo Charlie's and was soon gone, lock, stock, and lobster tank. As the pendulum swung back in the direction of less adventuresome palates, the same location became, for a time at least, the home of Country Bumpkin's, whose name alone suggested all that need be said about its cuisine.

Although I was satisfied that the opening of a McDonald's meant my hometown had definitely arrived, even I was surprised that a Wal-Mart opened in Hartwell shortly thereafter. More than any comparable business enterprise, a Wal-Mart store seems to bring dramatic changes to the shape and pace of community life. Once a center of social as well as economic activity, especially on Saturdays, downtown streets and the courthouse square are noticeably quieter because many shoppers have already made their purchases at Wal-Mart, which not only offers lower prices and wider selections (plus a snack bar) but also stays open all night. The result is a fundamental alteration in many traditional patterns of economic and social interaction, especially if the store is one of Georgia's more than one hundred Wal-Mart Supercenters, which offer just about everything, from work clothes to flat-screen televisions, not to mention glasses, gasoline, and groceries.

In fast-growing Cherokee County, however, Mary Hood found that Wal-Mart could actually be a metaphor for either continuity or change and sometimes for both. In a more rural section of the county, Hood found a Wal-Mart where the clerks had names like "Delma or Edna or Frony or Bud, Jr., and they call me m'am or honey." In this store's electronics department, the radios played country music and announced obituaries and car washes, while customers paid in cash, renewed old acquaintances, and parted company with "that country benediction, 'Y'all come to see us sometime.'" Nine miles away, Hood visited a second Wal-Mart reflective of the local community's transition from small town to suburb. At this establishment, the pace was faster and the snack bar nonexistent. "These are busy people, involved in PTA and soccer and tennis camp. . . . Everyone has somewhere else to be and soon." Here the radios blared 96 Rock, and most of the shoppers paid with "designer checks." The more youthful customers sported names such as Brandon and Angie and Kim and Scott and Amber, and among them, "orthodontia is epidemic." In a Wal-Mart even farther out, where the suburbs had actually roared past the little towns and reconfigured the pasture-lands, nothing or no one seemed at all tied to the locality itself. Here, Hood shopped in that "anonymity attained more often in large cities," and the clerks seemed more "worldly" and "chic." Though only a few miles from the cozy pay-cash ambiance of the first store, here Hood felt not just alienated but "underdressed" and had to remind herself, "My plastic's as good as theirs: I can owe for anything in this store." As if to affirm Hood's observations about Wal-Mart's capacity to adapt to local economic and social patterns even as it was simultaneously reshaping them, by the 1990s Wal-Mart had become for 68 percent of an *Atlanta Journal-Constitution* poll's respondents "very" or at least "somewhat" important to their definition of "today's South."

Although evidence of change abounded throughout twenty-first-century Georgia, those who looked closely could also find that the old ways had not entirely disappeared. Doubtless, many a tourist has been mystified, amused, or aggravated by the persistence of the old custom of pulling off the road and stopping the car while a funeral procession passes by. Whenever I encounter this practice, especially in busier metropolitan locales where one least expects to see it, I am always gratified, for it suggests that the personalism and caring that were fundamental elements of southern life at its best are with us yet, even as expressways, malls, and condominiums threaten to make us strangers in our own land.

Proper respect for funeral processions is only part of the appropriate ritual surrounding what a friend of mine calls the "southern way of death." Food plays an even more integral role. Bereaved loved ones are swamped with it as soon as word of their loss begins to spread. Organized by Sunday school classes, the ladies of the church show up without fanfare and prepare meals for the grieving family, offering hugs, condolences, and tender recollections of the departed. Through these acts of compassion and their dishes of potato salad and macaroni and cheese, they not only express sympathy and love but offer the comfort that only a sense of belonging to a community can bring. I have attended many funerals at the Cedar Creek Baptist Church (where I became the Georgia Baptist that, at heart, I will always be). Despite the sadness that I feel, I always come away with a better sense of who I am, because, on these occasions at least, the old world in which I grew up is still there, and even after all my wanderings, I still feel a part of it.

A CULTURAL COLLAGE

The constantly shifting cultural landscape of modern Georgia presented a jumbled panorama of anachronism, contradiction, contrast, and peculiarity, a delight to observe but a nightmare to explain or even describe. For example, John Berendt effectively immortalized the insularity and urban eccentricity of Savannah in *Midnight in the Garden of*

Good and Evil. Based on an actual murder case, Berendt's tale involved a controversial though socially prominent antiques dealer, a black transvestite known as the Lady Chablis, a voodoo priestess, and an offbeat inventor who was obsessed with finding a way to make goldfish glow in the dark.

Eccentricity was hardly unknown in the Georgia countryside either. Nobody gets into the holiday spirit quite like the exuberant participants in the annual Rock Branch Christmas parade, also known as the Bullsnort Christmas parade because it actually begins in the rural community of Bullsnort and concludes in the Elbert County microhamlet of Rock Branch. With a sometimes-ragged processional stretching out over several miles of spectator-lined country roads, the decidedly offbeat parade is open to anyone on foot, astride any kind of animal, or in any vehicle or conveyance, clean or dirty, decorated or not, be it an antique tractor or a brand new backhoe. Elsewhere, the unflattering historical stereotype of down-and-out Georgians eating clay, or "chalk," as it is known thereabouts, has not deterred the folks in Washington County (where kaolin producers reportedly pay more than half the ad valorem taxes) from holding an annual Kaolin Festival. Because the practice, while still not unknown, is severely stigmatized, there is no clay-eating contest, but the event features a parade and a crafts fair, and local beauties vie for the title of Kaolin Festival Queen.

Georgia's musical landscape, meanwhile, has only grown steadily richer and more diverse. The phenomenally popular R.E.M. has long since established Athens as a magnet for musicians and musical groupies from all over the world, and other local groups like Widespread Panic and the B-52's command a devoted following as well. Athens is also the birthplace and unofficial home base of Southern Rock sensations the Drive-By Truckers, whose songs often deal with the down-on-their-luck and desperate southerners whose stories are nowhere to be found in the grand narrative of Sunbelt-era success and prosperity.

Georgians like Monticello's Trisha Yearwood continue to make impressive contributions to the country music scene, but none of them have outshone Newnan native Alan Jackson. Jackson's phenomenal popularity rests in his unaffected country-boy sincerity and his ability to offer a fresh new sound while remaining true to the gritty, emotional themes and traditions that have always been at the heart of country music's message. Jackson told a story familiar to many small-town Georgians when he waxed nostalgic about "The Little Man" who once "pumped your gas" and "cleaned your glass" until his little filling station could no longer compete with corporate-owned convenience stores because "he couldn't sell slurpees" and he "wouldn't sell beer."

Like the city, Atlanta's rap scene has redefined itself repeatedly. Already known as the home of groups like OutKast and Goodie Mob, beginning in the mid-1990s Atlanta emerged as the capital of the Dirty South sound. Instead of apologizing for where they came from, Dirty South pioneers OutKast declared, "The South got somethin' to say!" Like many southern blacks in general, Killer Mike and other Dirty South performers embraced their regional roots with defiance and pride, asserting the southernness of their blackness as they sang the praises of soul food and asked, "If we cotton pickers, what better thing to be?"

For those who fancied themselves somewhat higher-browed, Augusta was home not only to the late Godfather of Soul but also to internationally acclaimed mezzo-soprano Jessye Norman. Meanwhile, the Atlanta Symphony Orchestra long ago achieved international prominence under the direction of the renowned former conductor Robert Shaw and has maintained its reputation under the leadership of Yoel Levi and Robert Spano.

Atlanta's commitment to the visual arts gave rise to and sustains the High Museum of Art, an imposing structure whose exhibits may, at any one time, feature sculpture from the Louvre or quilts from Alabama. Georgia has produced a good share of highly regarded artists, none of them more remarkable than painter Benny Andrews, one of ten children born to a black sharecropper family near Madison (Andrews's father, George, was also a talented artist and his aforementioned brother

Raymond, a well-known writer). Andrews's most highly regarded works presented large-scale portrayals of black and white life in rural Georgia. One of Georgia's most famous artists in the post–World War II era was Rev. Howard Finster, whose rustic and eccentric creations reflected the influence of the divine visions Finster claimed to have received regularly. A painter and sculptor, Finster adorned his work with scriptural admonitions and proverbs. Fittingly enough, the High Museum has acquired a sizable amount of Finster's work from his two-acre Paradise Garden near Summerville.

"GEORGIAN AS HELL"

In the wake of the 1996 Olympics, Atlanta, with Georgia in unsteady tow, seemed to have taken yet another giant step toward both the mass-society acceptance that many Georgians have sought for so long and the ultimate surrender to the relentless forces of homogenization and assimilation that others have simultaneously sought to forestall. In fact, even some of those who have expressed great pride in Georgia's role in leading the rest of the South toward the mainstream of American life have nonetheless fretted that their once-wayward state's baptism in this mainstream may wash away not only many of its sins but also some of its most vital and affirmative traits as well. In other words, like the late Mr. Grizzard, they fear that the social and economic changes once thought necessary for Georgia's salvation may, paradoxically enough, actually wind up destroying its soul.

Such worries did not disappear, but they did not appear to be a paramount concern for most Georgians. In keeping with a twenty-year trend showing a solid majority of those polled to be at least moderately pleased with their lives and their future prospects, a statewide survey in 2005 indicated that 64 percent of the 803 participants were at least moderately satisfied with the way things are going in Georgia. More whites (70 percent) seemed pleased than blacks, but 53 percent of the black respondents also expressed their satisfaction. Most longtime

Georgians clearly did not see eye-to-eye with the "livability" experts who ranked their state thirty-eighth in this category in 2005, and neither did the newcomers who made Georgia the nation's fourth-fastest-growing state in 2006.

Additional polling data indicates that most people in the state actually considered its almost explosive population growth a definite plus. There is clearly quite a difference between coming to Georgia and becoming a Georgian, of course. In 1990 only 64 percent of the residents of Georgia had actually been born here, and ten years later that figure was down to 58 percent. Meanwhile, scarcely a third of the population in faster-growing metropolitan counties like Cobb and Gwinnett were native Georgians in 2000.

In the face of this trend, one might suppose that the percentage of residents who feel any real sense of identification with the state can do nothing but shrink. On the other hand, we have seen repeatedly in recent years that the tendency of globalization to blur the distinctions among nations has often strengthened rather than eroded local and regional attachments. Online forums reveal a variety of initial reactions among newcomers to Georgia, including some dismay at the pervasive religious and political conservatism and the occasional homesickness for the supposedly greater diversity and dynamism of the West Coast or the Northeast. Among those who have been here a little while, however, the consensus seems to be "you'll get used to it" or "it'll grow on you." There is certainly reason to hope, therefore, that growing numbers of naturalized Georgians will become more comfortable with their state and their place within it, learning, as Faulkner suggested, to embrace it not only *because* but *despite*.

This may also be a case where succeeding generations, who, unlike their parents, were either born or at least grew up here, show greater attachment to Georgia than do Mom and Dad. Thanks in no small part to in-migration, the state ranked third in the nation in 2000 in the percentage of residents in the prime child-bearing age group comprised of twenty-five- to forty-four-year-olds, and its under-twenty population was projected to exceed one-third of the total by 2015. Granted, not many of tomorrow's Georgians are likely to match the fervor of the aforementioned old tobacco farmer who proclaimed himself "Georgian as hell," but then, seventy years ago, his defiantly provincial disdain for outsiders and knee-jerk resistance to change reflected not so much pride as an ill-concealed inferiority complex rooted in a still not-so-distant past shaped by poverty, division, and defeat. Perhaps coming generations will be able to draw on a more upbeat recent history marked by greater prosperity, tolerance, and achievement and find the confidence to live comfortably and productively in a more diverse and dynamic society where change is less a prospect than a certainty. If so, the designation "Georgian" will reflect no mere accident of race, gender, or geography but will belong to everybody who has chosen not only to become a part of Georgia as a political entity but to acknowledge that, as a compelling physical and communal presence, Georgia has become a part of them as well.

Bibliography

BIOGRAPHY/AUTOBIOGRAPHY

Anderson, William. *The Wild Man from Sugar Creek: The Political Career of Eugene Talmadge*. Baton Rouge: Louisiana State University Press, 1975.

Bell, Malcolm. *Major Butler's Legacy: Five Generations of a Slaveholding Family*. Athens: University of Georgia Press, 1987.

Bragg, William Harris. *De Renne: Three Generations of a Georgia Family*. Athens: University of Georgia Press, 1999.

Burns, Robert E. *I Am a Fugitive from a Georgia Chain Gang!* 1932. Reprint, Athens: University of Georgia Press, 1997.

Caldwell, Erskine. *With All My Might: An Autobiography*. Atlanta: Peachtree Publishers, 1987.

Carr, Virginia. *The Lonely Hunter: A Biography of Carson McCullers*. 1976. Reprint, Athens: University of Georgia Press, 2003.

Carter, Jimmy. *Keeping Faith: Memoirs of a President*. 1982. Reprint, Fayetteville: University of Arkansas Press, 1995.

―――. *Turning Point: A Candidate, a State, and a Nation Come of Age*. New York: Times Books, 1992.

Coles, Robert. *Flannery O'Connor's South*. 1980. Reprint, Athens: University of Georgia Press, 1993.

Cook, James F. *Carl Sanders: Spokesman of the New South*. Macon, Ga.: Mercer University Press, 1993.

————. *The Governors of Georgia, 1754–2004*. Macon, Ga.: Mercer University Press, 2005.

Cousins, Paul M. *Joel Chandler Harris: A Biography*. Baton Rouge: Louisiana State University Press, 1968.

Craft, William, and Ellen Craft. *Running a Thousand Miles for Freedom: The Escape of William and Ellen Craft from Slavery*. 1860. Reprint, Athens: University of Georgia Press, 1999.

Crews, Harry. *A Childhood: The Biography of a Place*. 1978. Reprint, Athens: University of Georgia Press, 1995.

Duncan, Russell. *Freedom's Shore: Tunis Campbell and the Georgia Freedmen*. Athens: University of Georgia Press, 1986.

Fite, Gilbert C. *Richard B. Russell, Jr., Senator from Georgia*. Chapel Hill: University of North Carolina Press, 1991.

Henderson, Harold P. *The Politics of Change in Georgia: A Political Biography of Ellis Arnall*. Athens: University of Georgia Press, 1991.

Hunter-Gault, Charlayne. *In My Place*. 1992. Reprint, New York: Vintage Books, 1993.

Leslie, Kent Anderson. *Woman of Color, Daughter of Privilege: Amanda America Dickson, 1849–1893*. Athens: University of Georgia Press, 1995.

Lewis, David L. *King: A Critical Biography*. New York: Praeger, 1970.

Lewis, John. *Walking with the Wind: A Memoir of the Movement*. New York: Simon and Schuster, 1998.

Loveland, Anne C. *Lillian Smith: A Southerner Confronting the South*. Baton Rouge: Louisiana State University Press, 1986.

Lumpkin, Katharine Du Pre. *The Making of a Southerner*. 1946. Reprint, Athens: University of Georgia Press, 1991.

Martin, Harold H. *William Berry Hartsfield, Mayor of Atlanta*. Athens: University of Georgia Press, 1978.

McGill, Ralph. *The South and the Southerner*. 1963. Reprint, Athens: University of Georgia Press, 1992.

Mixon, Wayne. *The People's Writer: Erskine Caldwell and the South*. Charlottesville: University Press of Virginia, 1995.

Pyron, Darden Asbury. *Southern Daughter: The Life of Margaret Mitchell*. New York: Oxford University Press, 1991.

Ray, Janisse. *Ecology of a Cracker Childhood*. Minneapolis: Milkweed Editions, 1999.

Smith, Lillian. *Killers of the Dream*. 1949. Reprint, Garden City, N.Y.: Doubleday, 1963.

Spalding, Phinizy. *Oglethorpe in America*. 1977. Reprint, Athens: University of Georgia Press, 1984.

Talmadge, John Erwin. *Rebecca Latimer Felton: Nine Stormy Decades*. Athens: University of Georgia Press, 1960.

White, Walter. *A Man Called White*. Athens: University of Georgia Press, 1995.

Woodward, C. Vann. *Tom Watson, Agrarian Rebel*. 1938. Reprint, New York: Oxford University Press, 1963.

Young, Andrew. *An Easy Burden: The Civil Rights Movement and the Transformation of America*. New York: HarperCollins, 1996.

FICTION

Andrews, Raymond. *Appalachee Red*. 1978. Reprint, Athens: University of Georgia Press, 1987.

Ansa, Tina McElroy. *Ugly Ways*. New York: Harcourt Brace and Company, 1993.

Berendt, John. *Midnight in the Garden of Good and Evil*. New York: Random House, 1994.

Blount, Roy, Jr. *Crackers: This Whole Many-Angled Thing of Jimmy, More Carters, Ominous Little Animals, Sad Singing Women, My Daddy, and Me*. New York: Alfred A. Knopf, 1980.

Burns, Olive Ann. *Cold Sassy Tree*. 1984. Reprint, Boston: Houghton Mifflin, 2007.

Caldwell, Erskine. *Tobacco Road*. 1932. Reprint, Athens: University of Georgia Press, 1995.

Crews, Harry. *A Feast of Snakes*. 1976. Reprint, New York: Scribner, 1998.

———. *The Gospel Singer*. 1968. Reprint, New York: Perennial Library, 1988.

Dickey, James. *Deliverance*. Boston: Houghton Mifflin, 1970.

Fields, Jeff. *A Cry of Angels: A Novel*. Athens: University of Georgia Press, 2006.

Harris, Corra. *A Circuit Rider's Wife*. Athens: University of Georgia Press, 1998.

Harris, Joel Chandler. *The Complete Tales of Uncle Remus*. Boston: Houghton Mifflin, 1955.

Kantor, MacKinlay. *Andersonville*. New York: Plume, 1993.

Kay, Terry. *The Year the Lights Came On*. 1976. Reprint, Athens: University of Georgia Press, 2007.

McCullers, Carson. *The Heart Is a Lonely Hunter*. 1940. Reprint, New York: Modern Library, 1993.

Miller, Caroline. *Lamb in His Bosom*. Atlanta: Peachtree Publishers, 1993.

Mitcham, Judson. *Sabbath Creek*. Athens: University of Georgia Press, 2004.

———. *The Sweet Everlasting*. Athens: University of Georgia Press, 1996.

Mitchell, Margaret. *Gone with the Wind*. 1936. Reprint, New York: Scribner, 1996.

Newman, Frances. *The Hard-Boiled Virgin*. 1926. Reprint, Athens: University of Georgia Press, 1994.

O'Connor, Flannery. *Everything That Rises Must Converge*. New York: Farrar, Straus and Giroux, 1965.

———. *Wise Blood: A Novel*. 1952. Reprint, New York: Farrar, Straus and Giroux, 2007.

Ruppersburg, Hugh, ed. *After O'Connor: Stories from Contemporary Georgia*. Athens: University of Georgia Press, 2003.

———, ed. *Georgia Voices. Vol. 1, Fiction*. Athens: University of Georgia Press, 1992.

———, ed. *The New Georgia Encyclopedia Companion to Georgia Literature*. Athens: University of Georgia Press, 2007.

Sams, Ferrol. *Run with the Horsemen*. Atlanta: Peachtree Publishers, 1982.

Siddons, Anne Rivers. *Peachtree Road*. New York: Harper and Row, 1988.

Simms, William Gilmore. *Guy Rivers: A Tale of Georgia*. Lenox, Mass.: Hard Press, 2006.

Smith, Lillian. *Strange Fruit*. 1944. Reprint, Athens: University of Georgia Press, 1985.

Toomer, Jean. *Cane*. 1923. New York: Penguin, 1999.

Uhry, Alfred. *Driving Miss Daisy*. New York: Theatre Communications Group, 1988.

Walker, Alice. *The Color Purple*. New York: Harcourt Brace Jovanovich, 1982.

White, Bailey. *Mama Makes Up Her Mind and Other Dangers of Southern Living*. Reading, Mass.: Addison-Wesley, 1993.

Wolfe, Tom. *A Man in Full*. 1998. Reprint, New York: Bantam, 2001.

FOLKLORE/FOLK ART/MUSIC

Bailey, Cornelia, and Christena Bledsoe. *God, Dr. Buzzard, and the Bolito Man: A Saltwater Geechee Talks about Life on Sapelo Island, Georgia*. New York: Anchor Books, 2001.

Burrison, John A. *Brothers in Clay: The Story of Georgia Folk Pottery*. Athens: University of Georgia Press, 1995.

Cobb, Buell E. *The Sacred Harp: A Tradition and Its Music*. Athens: University of Georgia Press, 1989.

Georgia Writers' Project. *Drums and Shadows: Survival Studies among the Georgia Coastal Negroes*. 1940. Reprint, Athens: University of Georgia Press, 1986.

Grem, Darren E. "'The South Got Something to Say': Atlanta's Dirty South and the Southernization of Hip-Hop America." *Southern Cultures* 12 (Winter 2006), 55–73.

Longstreet, Augustus Baldwin. *Georgia Scenes*. Whitefish, Mont.: Kessinger Publishing, 2004.

Mariella, Glenn Hartsfield. *Tall Betsy and Dunce Baby: South Georgia Folktales*. Athens: University of Georgia Press, 1987.

Rosenbaum, Art, and Johann S. Buis. *Shout Because You're Free: The African American Ring Shout Tradition in Coastal Georgia*. Athens: University of Georgia Press, 1998.

Wigginton, Eliot, et al., eds., *Foxfire* Series, 12 vols. Various publishers, 1972-present.

GENERAL REFERENCE

Coleman, Kenneth, et al. *A History of Georgia*. 2nd ed. Athens: University of Georgia Press, 1991.

Coleman, Kenneth, and Charles Stephen Gurr, eds. *Dictionary of Georgia Biography*. 2 vols. Athens: University of Georgia Press, 1983.

Georgia Statistics Systems. http://www.georgiastats.uga.edu.

Georgia: The WPA Guide to its Towns and Countryside. Introduction by Phinizy Spalding. 1940. Reprint, Columbia: University of South Carolina Press, 1990.

Hepburn, Lawrence R., ed. *Contemporary Georgia*. 2nd ed. Athens: Carl Vinson Institute of Government, University of Georgia, 1992.

The New Georgia Encyclopedia. www.georgiaencyclopedia.org.

The New Georgia Guide. Athens: University of Georgia Press, 1996.

Range, Willard. *A Century of Georgia Agriculture, 1850–1950*. Athens: University of Georgia Press, 1954.

Ruppersburg, Hugh, ed. *Georgia Voices. Vol. 2: Nonfiction*. Athens: University of Georgia Press, 1994.

Scott, Thomas A. *Cornerstones of Georgia History: Documents that Formed the State*. Athens: University of Georgia Press, 1995.

HIGHER EDUCATION

Coulter, E. Merton. *College Life in the Old South*. 1951. Reprint, Athens: University of Georgia Press, 1983.

Dickey, Ouida, and Doyle Mathis. *Berry College: A History*. Athens: University of Georgia Press, 2005.

Dyer, Thomas G. *The University of Georgia: A Bicentennial History, 1785–1985*. Athens: University of Georgia Press, 1985.

Hawk, Gary S. *A Legacy of Heart and Mind: Emory Since 1836*. Atlanta: Emory University, 1999.

McMath, Robert C., Jr., et al. *Engineering the New South: Georgia Tech, 1885–1985*. Athens: University of Georgia Press, 1985.

Pratt, Robert A. *We Shall Not Be Moved: The Desegregation of the University of Georgia*. Athens: University of Georgia Press, 2005.

Trillin, Calvin. *An Education in Georgia: Charlayne Hunter, Hamilton Holmes, and the Integration of the University of Georgia*. 1964. Reprint, Athens: University of Georgia Press, 1991.

Anderson, William L., ed. *Cherokee Removal: Before and After*. Athens: University of Georgia Press, 1991.

Cashin, Edward J., ed. *A Wilderness Still the Cradle of Nature: Frontier Georgia, a Documentary History*. Savannah: Library of Georgia, 1994.

Hudson, Charles M. *The Southeastern Indians*. Knoxville: University of Tennessee Press, 1976.

Perdue, Theda, and Michael D. Green. *The Cherokee Removal: A Brief History with Documents*. 2nd ed., Boston: Bedford Books, 2005.

HISTORY: COLONIAL/REVOLUTIONARY

Abbott, William W. *The Royal Governors of Georgia, 1754–1775*. Chapel Hill: University of North Carolina Press, 1959.

Bonner, James C. *A History of Georgia Agriculture, 1732–1860*. Athens: University of Georgia Press, 1964.

Cashin, Edward J. *Governor Henry Ellis and the Transformation of British North America*. Athens: University of Georgia Press, 1994.

———. *Lachlan McGillivray, Indian Trader: The Shaping of the Southern Colonial Frontier*. Athens: University of Georgia Press, 1992.

Coleman, Kenneth. *The American Revolution in Georgia: 1763–1789*. Athens: University of Georgia Press, 1958.

———. *Colonial Georgia: A History*. New York: Charles Scribner and Sons, 1976.

Davis, Harold Earl. *The Fledgling Province: Social and Cultural Life in Colonial Georgia, 1733–1776*. Chapel Hill: University of North Carolina Press, 1976.

Gallay, Alan, ed. *Voices of the Old South: Eyewitness Accounts, 1528–1861*. Athens: University of Georgia Press, 1994.

Jackson, Harvey H. *Lachlan McIntosh and the Politics of Revolutionary Georgia*. Athens: University of Georgia Press, 2003.

———, and Phinizy Spalding. *Forty Years of Diversity: Essays on Colonial Georgia*. Athens: University of Georgia Press, 1984.

Lockley, Timothy. *Lines in the Sand: Race and Class in Lowcountry Georgia, 1750–1860*. Athens: University of Georgia Press, 2004.

Marsh, Ben. *Georgia's Frontier Women: Female Fortunes in a Southern Colony*. Athens: University of Georgia Press, 2007.

Smith, Julia Floyd. *Slavery and Rice Culture in Low Country Georgia, 1750–1860*. Knoxville: University of Tennessee Press, 1985.

Sweet, Julie Ann. *Negotiating for Georgia: British-Creek Relations in the Trustee Era, 1733–1752*. Athens: University of Georgia Press, 2005.

Wood, Betty. *Slavery in Colonial Georgia, 1730–1775*. Athens: University of Georgia Press, 1984.

HISTORY: ANTEBELLUM

Carey, Anthony Gene. *Parties, Slavery, and the Union in Antebellum Georgia*. Athens: University of Georgia Press, 1997.

Fraser, Walter J., Jr. *Savannah in the Old South*. Athens: University of Georgia Press, 2005.

Freehling, William W., and Craig M. Simpson, eds. *Secession Debated: Georgia's Showdown in 1860*. New York: Oxford University Press, 1992.

Gillespie, Michele. *Free Labor in an Unfree World: White Artisans in Slaveholding Georgia, 1789–1860*. Athens: University of Georgia Press, 2004.

Kemble, Frances Anne. *Journal of a Residence on a Georgia Plantation in 1838–1839*. Athens: University of Georgia Press, 1984.

Reidy, Joseph P. *From Slavery to Agrarian Capitalism in the Cotton Plantation South: Central Georgia, 1800–1880*. Chapel Hill: University of North Carolina Press, 1992.

Williams, David. *The Georgia Gold Rush: Twenty-niners, Cherokees, and Gold Fever*. Columbia: University of South Carolina Press, 1993.

HISTORY: CIVIL WAR/RECONSTRUCTION

Andrews, Eliza Frances. *The War-Time Journal of a Georgia Girl, 1864–1865*. 1908. Reprint, Atlanta: Cherokee Publishing Company, 1976.

Boney, F. N. *Rebel Georgia*. Macon, Ga.: Mercer University Press, 1997.

DeCredico, Mary A. *Patriotism for Profit: Georgia's Urban Entrepreneurs and the Confederate War Effort*. Chapel Hill: University of North Carolina Press, 1990.

Drago, Edmund L. *Black Politicians and Reconstruction in Georgia: A Splendid Failure.* 1982. Reprint, Athens: University of Georgia Press, 1992.

Dyer, Thomas G. *Secret Yankees: The Union Circle in Confederate Atlanta.* Baltimore, Md.: Johns Hopkins University Press, 1999.

Flynn, Charles L., Jr. *White Land, Black Labor: Caste and Class in Late Nineteenth-Century Georgia.* Baton Rouge: Louisiana State University Press, 1983.

Foner, Eric. *Reconstruction: America's Unfinished Reconstruction, 1867–1877.* New York: Harper and Row, 1988.

Glatthaar, Joseph T. *The March to the Sea and Beyond: Sherman's Troops in the Savannah and Carolina Campaigns.* Baton Rouge: Louisiana State University Press, 1995.

Hahn, Steven. *The Roots of Southern Populism: Yeoman Farmers and the Transformation of the Georgia Upcountry, 1850–1890,* updated ed. New York: Oxford University Press, 2006.

Johnson, Michael P. *Toward a Patriarchal Republic: The Secession of Georgia.* Baton Rouge: Louisiana State University Press, 1977.

Jones, Jacqueline. *Soldiers of Light and Love: Northern Teachers and Georgia Blacks, 1865–1873.* Reprint, Athens: University of Georgia Press, 1992.

Kennett, Lee B. *Marching through Georgia: The Story of Soldiers and Civilians during Sherman's Campaign.* New York: Harper Collins, 1995.

Lane, Mills. *Standing upon the Mouth of a Volcano: New South Georgia, a Documentary History.* Savannah, Ga.: Beehive Press, 1993.

———. *Times That Prove People's Principles: Civil War in Georgia, a Documentary History.* Savannah, Ga.: Beehive Press, 1993.

Leigh, Frances Butler. *Ten Years on a Georgia Plantation since the War, 1866–1876.* 1969. Reprint, Savannah, Ga.: Beehive Foundation, 1992.

Marvel, William. *Andersonville: The Last Depot.* Chapel Hill: University of North Carolina Press, 2006.

McFeely, William S. *Sapelo's People: A Long Walk into Freedom.* New York: W.W. Norton and Company, 1994.

Mohr, Clarence L. *On the Threshold of Freedom: Masters and Slaves in Civil War Georgia.* Athens: University of Georgia Press, 1986.

Myers, Robert Manson, ed. *The Children of Pride: Selected Letters of the Family of the Rev. Dr. Charles Colcock Jones from the Years 1860–1868.* New Haven: Yale University Press, 1984.

O'Donovan, Susan Eva. *Becoming Free in the Cotton South.* Cambridge: Harvard University Press, 2007.

Phillips, Ulrich B., ed. *The Correspondence of Robert Toombs, Alexander H. Stephens, and Howell Cobb.* 1911. Reprint, New York: Da Capo Press, 1970.

Sarris, Jonathan Dean. *A Separate Civil War: Communities in Conflict in the Mountain South.* Charlottesville: University of Virginia Press, 2006.

Wetherington, Mark V. *The New South Comes to Wiregrass Georgia, 1860–1910.* Knoxville: University of Tennessee Press, 1994.

Williams, David, Teresa Crisp Williams, and David Carlson. *Plain Folk in a Rich Man's War: Class and Dissent in Confederate Georgia.* Gainesville: University Press of Florida, 2002.

HISTORY: LATE NINETEENTH / EARLY TWENTIETH CENTURY

Brundage, W. Fitzhugh. *Lynching in the New South: Georgia and Virginia, 1880–1930.* Urbana: University of Illinois Press, 1993.

Chirhart, Ann Short. *Torches of Light: Georgia Teachers and the Coming of the Modern South.* Athens: University of Georgia Press, 2005.

Dinnerstein, Leonard. *The Leo Frank Case,* rev. ed. Athens: University of Georgia Press, 2008.

Dittmer, John. *Black Georgia in the Progressive Era, 1900–1920.* Urbana: University of Illinois Press, 1977.

Flamming, Douglas. *Creating the Modern South: Millhands and Managers in Dalton, Georgia, 1884–1984.* Chapel Hill: University of North Carolina Press, 1992.

Godschalk, David. *Veiled Visions: The 1906 Atlanta Race Riot and the Reshaping of American Race Relations.* Chapel Hill: University of North Carolina Press, 2005.

Goodson, Steve. *Highbrows, Hillbillies, and Hellfire: Public Entertainment in Atlanta, 1880–1930.* Athens: University of Georgia Press, 2007.

Holmes, William F., ed. *Struggling to Shake Off Old Shackles: Twentieth-Century Georgia, a Documentary History.* Savannah, Ga.: Beehive Press, 1995.

Inscoe, John C., ed. *Georgia in Black and White: Explorations in the Race Relations of a Southern State, 1865–1950.* Athens: University of Georgia Press, 1994.

MacLean, Nancy. *Behind the Mask of Chivalry: The Making of the Second Ku Klux Klan*. New York: Oxford University Press, 1995.

Oney, Steve. *And the Dead Shall Rise: The Murder of Mary Phagan and the Lynching of Leo Frank*. New York: Vintage, 2004.

Schultz, Mark Roman. *The Rural Face of White Supremacy: Beyond Jim Crow*. Urbana: University of Illinois Press, 2006.

Shaw, Barton C. *The Wool-Hat Boys: Georgia's Populist Party*. Baton Rouge: Louisiana State University Press, 1984.

Wexler, Laura. *Fire in a Canebrake: The Last Mass Lynching in America*. New York: Scribner, 2003.

Woodward, C. Vann. *Tom Watson, Agrarian Rebel*. 1938. Reprint, New York: Oxford University Press, 1963.

HISTORY: POST–WORLD WAR II

Bartley, Numan V. *The Creation of Modern Georgia*. 2nd ed. Athens: University of Georgia Press, 1990.

Branch, Taylor. *At Canaan's Edge: America in the King Years, 1965–68*. New York: Simon and Schuster, 2007.

———. *Parting the Waters: America in the King Years, 1954–63*. New York: Simon and Schuster, 1988.

———. *Pillar of Fire: America in the King Years, 1963–65*. New York: Simon and Schuster, 1999.

Egerton, John. *Speak Now against the Day: The Generation before the Civil Rights Movement in the South*. New York: Alfred A. Knopf, 1994.

Fite, Gilbert C. *Richard B. Russell, Jr., Senator from Georgia*. Chapel Hill: University of North Carolina Press, 1991.

Green, Melissa Fay. *Praying for Sheetrock*. New York: Ballantine Books, 1991.

———. *The Temple Bombing*. New York: Da Capo Press, 2006.

Hatfield, Edward A. "MARTA and the Making of Suburban Conservatism." M.A. Thesis. University of Georgia, 2006.

Tuck, Stephen. *Beyond Atlanta: The Struggle for Racial Equality in Georgia, 1940–1980*. Athens: University of Georgia Press, 2003.

Watters, Pat. *Down to Now: Reflections on the Southern Civil Rights Movement*. 1971. Reprint, Athens: University of Georgia Press, 1993.

LOCAL/REGIONAL/ATLANTA

Allen, Frederick. *Atlanta Rising: The Invention of an International City, 1946–1996.* Atlanta: Longstreet Press, 1996.

Bayor, Ronald H. *Race and the Shaping of Twentieth-Century Atlanta.* Chapel Hill: University of North Carolina Press, 1996.

Crimmins, Timothy, and Anne Farrisee. *Democracy Restored: A History of the Georgia State Capitol.* Athens: University of Georgia Press, 2007.

Davis, Harold Eugene. *Henry Grady's New South: Atlanta, a Brave and Beautiful City.* Tuscaloosa: University of Alabama Press, 1990.

Dorsey, Allison. *To Build Our Lives Together: Community Formation in Black Atlanta, 1875–1906.* Athens: University of Georgia Press, 2004.

Pomerantz, Gary. *Where Peachtree Meets Sweet Auburn: The Saga of Two Families and the Making of Atlanta.* New York: Scribner, 1996.

LOCAL/REGIONAL/ALL OTHER REGIONS

Berendt, John. *Midnight in the Garden of Good and Evil.* New York: Random House, 1994.

Bullard, Mary R. *Cumberland Island: A History.* Athens: University of Georgia Press, 2005.

Cashin, Edward J., and Glenn T. Eskew, eds. *Paternalism in a Southern City: Race, Religion, and Gender in Augusta, Georgia.* Athens: University of Georgia Press, 2001.

Manis, Andrew M. *Macon Black and White: An Unutterable Separation in the American Century.* Macon, Ga.: Mercer University Press, 2004.

Miller, Zell Bryan. *The Mountains within Me.* 1976. Reprint, Atlanta, Ga.: Cherokee Publishing Company, 1985.

Nelson, Megan Kate. *Trembling Earth: A Cultural History of the Okefenokee Swamp.* Athens: University of Georgia Press, 2005.

Stewart, Mart A. *"What Nature Suffers to Groe": Life, Labor, and Landscape on the Georgia Coast, 1680–1920.* Athens: University of Georgia Press, 1996.

Thomas, Frances Taliaferro. *A Portrait of Historic Athens and Clarke County.* Athens: University of Georgia Press, 1992.

Index